PRAISE FOR *CUSTO*
TRANSFORMATION

'For anyone who seeks to improve their services, let this book be your design-led guide. It will enable you to truly transform your services by staging engaging, personal and memorable – even beautiful – experiences.' **B Joseph Pine II, co-author,** *The Experience Economy*

'This book is grounded in reality – it provides a vision, as well as practical strategies, for companies to embed design-led change across their business.' **Katy Pearce, Global Head of Customer Experience, Vodafone Group Enterprise**

'This will be my go-to book whenever I'm shaping new customer experience initiatives. It is a how-to guide for any customer experience team in any industry. Brilliant.' **John Patterson, Vice President of Customer Experience, Sage**

'Design's insight into customers' perspectives is the grit in the oyster that leads to great services. Here, Joe Heapy, Oliver King and James Samperi use their 20 years of experience at the forefront of applying design to services to help you understand the challenges and derive superb solutions. In the age of social media, shoddy services cannot survive; the distilled wisdom in this book will help you get the thumbs up, not the thumbs down.' **Bruce Tether, Professor of Innovation Management, Alliance Manchester Business School, University of Manchester**

'A really thorough book by well-informed authors, getting into the nitty-gritty of making service design happen in your organization.' **Kai En Ong, Head of User Experience and Design, BBC**

'Design thinking effectively provides a structure – a scaffold – that shapes the process of service development and guides teams to effective, beautiful and desirable service provision. This book is an aide-memoire and a guide to a process. The end-user-centricity and the passion that it invokes are key. I will keep *Customer-Driven Transformation* by my side as a reference and a guide.' **Andreas Tsiotsias, CTO, Computer Services Industry, IBM**

'This is an exceptional book. It's written in a pragmatic and action-oriented style, directed at "game changers" working in the field of services development and management, at a time where customer experience is key to creating lasting competitive advantage.' **Francisco Vieira Pita, Aviation Marketing Director, ANA – Aeroportos de Portugal**

'Finding a book that's filled with practical tips and stories from other customer experience leaders serves to reassure us that every organization's journey is unique and that we need to adapt. I wish I'd had this book 10 years ago.' **Hazel Hughes, Customer Experience and Operations Director, Weight Watchers UK**

'Delivering better services for customers can often feel like a daily battle within big organizations – but it's a battle worth having. This book provides you with all the tips, tools and techniques you need to instigate culture change outside of the design team.' **Kate Kapp, Head of Service Design, Tesco PLC**

'The design of the services we interact with each day is critical in the ever more competitive world of brands vying for our loyalty. And if those services stretch across a multitude of channels, the complexity of delivering customer delight consistently can become bewildering. Enter the experts! Engine Service Design has consistently proven the effectiveness of their solutions to complex problems, not only delivering great customer service but in adding tangible value to the brands they work with. Being able to get the inside line on their know-how is invaluable – and *Customer-Driven Transformation* the foundation stone to building great brand experiences.' **Deborah Dawton, CEO, Design Business Association, UK**

'Being a disruptor or coping with disruption are the challenges all business leaders face. In *Customer-Driven Transformation*, the authors put a spotlight on the excuses that stop people building their path to success. This is a must-read for all contemporary managers.' **Rashik Parmar MBE FBCS, IBM Distinguished Engineer and Technical Executive, Europe**

Customer-Driven Transformation

How being design-led helps companies get the right services to market

Joe Heapy
Oliver King
James Samperi

KoganPage

First published in Great Britain and the United States in 2018 by Kogan Page Limited

2nd Floor, 45 Gee Street	c/o Martin P Hill Consulting	4737/23 Ansari Road
London	122 W 27th St, 10th Floor	Daryaganj
EC1V 3RS	New York, NY 10001	New Delhi 110002
United Kingdom	USA	India

www.koganpage.com

© Engine Service Design, 2018

ISBN   978 0 7494 8301 2
E-ISBN   978 0 7494 8302 9

British Library Cataloguing-in-Publication Data

A CIP record for this book is available from the British Library.

Library of Congress Cataloging-in-Publication Data

Names: Heapy, Joe, author. | King, Oliver (Business consultant), author. | Samperi, James, author.
Title: Customer-driven transformation : how being design-led helps companies get the right services to market / Joe Heapy, Oliver King and James Samperi.
Description: London ; New York : Kogan Page, 2018. | Includes bibliographical references and index.
Identifiers: LCCN 2018024735 (print) | LCCN 2018026926 (ebook) | ISBN 9780749483029 (ebook) | ISBN 9780749483012 (pbk.)
Subjects: LCSH: Customer services. | New products. | Service industries.
Classification: LCC HF5415.5 (ebook) | LCC HF5415.5 .H38834 2018 (print) | DDC 658.8/12–dc23

Typeset by Integra Software Services, Pondicherry
Print production managed by Jellyfish
Printed and bound by CPI Group (UK) Ltd, Croydon, CR0 4YY

CONTENTS

13   Think like a Designer 169

Conclusion 187

To access additional resources please go to:

www.koganpage.com/CDT

or:

www.customerdrivenbook.com

ABOUT THE AUTHORS

Joe Heapy is co-founder and director of Engine Service Design. With roots in industrial product design, Joe is an advocate of the social value of design in improving people's lives. He's worked with clients across many sectors to help them improve their business performance and the way their customers experience their services. In 2006 Joe collaborated with the public policy think tank Demos to research and publish *The Journey to the Interface*, one of the first publications to describe the application of design school-trained user-centred design methods to the design of public services. He's an Honorary Professor of Design at Glasgow School of Art and a Visiting Professor at the Royal College of Art in London.

Oliver King is also co-founder and director of Engine. Oliver helps organizations identify where, when and how they can provide better, more meaningful and more valuable services. He is a passionate advocate of co-creation and design thinking, and of helping organizations improve their own design capabilities. Oliver works across all sectors but has extensive experience in travel, automotive, hospitality and energy. He's a recognized pioneer in his field and regularly speaks and writes internationally about service design and innovation. He's also a Board Director of the UK Design Business Association.

James Samperi is a director of Engine and has a background in industrial product design, design research and design strategy. He's responsible for the delivery of Engine's projects across all sectors, including the design and development of services for Mercedes-Benz, E.ON, Channel 4, Dubai Airports and the BBC. James has worked in agencies and as a client of service design in large organizations and, as a result, has a strong appreciation of what it takes to deliver great products and services. He now runs Engine's largest Dubai-based programme of work. As part of this work, James acted as the client organization's interim Head of Customer Experience and continues to manage the programme from Engine's studio in Dubai. He regularly speaks about and runs training in service design and its impact on business.

Acknowledgement We'd like to thank the Engine team for their enthusiasm, ideas and contributions to the development of our practice and to this book.

ABOUT THE CONTRIBUTORS

One of the most enjoyable aspects of writing this book has been the excuse to get our clients and ex-clients involved too. We, like so many organizations, often don't make the most of feedback and reflection and doing so has been an important motivator for us. Rather than writing formal case studies, woven through the chapters are anecdotes and points of view from eleven contributors, all of whom we've delivered projects with in the two years prior to this book being published. The objectives and outcomes of these projects have been as diverse as the organizations we've worked with, but each contributor has experienced a service design project and each has commissioned and delivered these projects with the parallel agenda of using design thinking and methods to get their organization thinking and working differently. All our contributors are talented and ambitious people, so some may have changed role and even employer since we spoke to them. Let's introduce them.

Adam Elliott was Head of Customer Experience Programme Development at National Grid. National Grid is responsible for the transmission of electricity and gas in the UK and is part of the National Grid Group, which also operates in parts of the US. Before we worked with him at National Grid, Adam was part of our client team at E.ON, first in the UK and subsequently at the European level, setting up a team and running projects to improve the experience for E.ON's customers. Adam is a seasoned customer experience professional, able to navigate the challenges of getting a movement started, and likes to use design thinking and tools to make things happen.

Sean Risebrow has been leading the customer experience agenda in the many businesses he's worked for in the last 15 years, probably longer. We first worked with Sean when he was at Virgin Media, which provides telephone, television and broadband internet services and is now part of the Liberty Global Group. It was early days for Virgin Media and Sean had been talking to the C-suite about the importance of improving the experience for Virgin Media's customers. He was given the challenge of demonstrating the impact this would have. We went on to work with the team there for four years on several projects. Sean then moved and moved again and we began working with him in his latest role for the health insurer and provider Bupa.

Samantha Murat has worked for some great service brands including Eurostar and Sainsbury's, one of the major grocers and now retail groups in the UK. We worked with Sam when she moved to a newly created position within Transport for London, which operates public transport across the capital. Sam describes some of the challenges of being in a customer experience role inside what is, in reality, an engineering business with a public service mandate. Despite its heritage, the organization has instigated significant changes to the experience of London's transport and to the organization itself as it faces up to the need to become self-funding.

Yeonhee Lee and **Stella Sangok** work for the Hyundai Motor Company in South Korea. As a global business the Company has big ambitions and wants to be the world's best for service in the automotive industry. We worked with Yeonhee and Stella to imagine and design a ground-breaking retail experience for the Company's new retail experience model, Hyundai Motorstudio in Gangnam, an upmarket district in the capital Seoul. A central part of the design of the experience was a consideration of the roles and behaviours of Hyundai people working and serving customers in this multi-story destination store.

Crispin Humm is Head of Journey at the UK Rail Delivery Group, which represents over 20 train operating companies and seeks to improve the service and customer experience for the whole rail network. We worked with Crispin and the team to envision and plan for improvements to the provision of customer information. Earlier in his career Crispin was an Officer in the British Army. During our conversations he compared the practices of military planning and achieving the mission with some of the tools and ideas from the design toolkit, specifically the need to communicate a clear vision and to assess how and when to deploy the resources you have at your disposal.

Keith Fletcher is Senior Customer Experience Change Programme Manager at E.ON Energy. Keith works with E.ON's business across Europe to implement the customer advocacy measure, Net Promotor, and propagate customer experience best practices. We'll discover later how E.ON has been training its people to think like Designers.

Johanna Jäkälä is CMO and VP Brand, Marketing & Customer Loyalty at the Finnish national airline, Finnair. Finnair operates from Helsinki Airport, which is operated by Finavia, and both organizations work very closely to deliver services and a great experience for passengers and visitors to the airport. Helsinki Airport works amazingly well; it's efficient, clean and reliable. Yet, like many airports, Helsinki competes for airlines' routes and for travelling passengers. As well as delivering improvements to the airport today, Finavia is investing in the development of new terminal buildings. We worked with Johanna and the team to imagine passenger services and an experience to match the amazing buildings they've already begun to construct.

Helen Woodrow was VP of Research at Dubai Airports until 2017. Helen wore several hats, leading both capacity and operational planning as well as customer experience. Her role focused on forecasting demand, defining capacity and experience requirements across multiple timeframes and identifying optimal solutions for enhancing capacity, efficiency and service levels. She led the development of Dubai Airports' customer experience strategy and established various projects, initiatives and ways of working to enhance the organization's research, understanding and responsiveness to customer needs and expectations across the vast and diverse customer base of Dubai International Airport.

Frank McCrorie is the Senior Vice President of Operations for Dubai Airports and is accountable for leading a team of over 800 staff including Terminal, Airside and Engineering Services. He is directly accountable for driving a sustained improvement in all operational areas including customer experience, safety and capacity in an increasingly constrained environment, whilst also delivering a business performance in line with expectations. He has been at the forefront of driving a culture of service through all his operational teams and continues to lead the development of sizable service improvement programmes across one of the world's busiest airports.

Clare Bacchus is the Customer Experience Director for PegasusLife, a property development business on a mission to rethink the way older people's housing is considered. We worked with Clare to create a new sales journey to move consumers away from just buying bricks and mortar to buying into a brand and service that reflects the lifestyles and aspirations of older people. As PegasusLife homes are often still under construction when they are bought, we needed to give the Sales Team the tools to bring the experience of living in a PegasusLife property... to life. We focused on ways to demonstrate PegasusLife's approach to apartment living, facilities, communities and services and how in combination these improve wellbeing and enjoyment for people over 65. The mission was to create brand advocates of PegasusLife before customers had even moved in to their homes and in turn drive commercial performance.

Introduction

We're all consumers of services and we all have an intuitive sense of what great service looks and feels like. Yet when it comes to our own customers, it's not at all obvious what they'll love and truly value, nor is it obvious how to shape organizations to get more of the right services to market.

If amazing services were easy for organizations to envision, create and deliver, think how wonderful our world would be. And consider how simple the life of a service provider would become, as designing and delivering a positive customer experience would be the work of minutes. As we know, we don't live in that kind of world. But that's no bad thing for you if you develop and deliver services, because you're about to learn how to get more of the right services to market faster.

By the end of this book you'll understand how to create the services your customers really want, so you can share this knowledge with others in your business. And if you run your own company, you'll have the insight you need to encourage your customers to return time and again.

If you think about it, we humans couldn't get far without services – they underpin almost everything in modern life. When we travel to a foreign country, we take a plane because we lack the wings to fly; when we want to talk to someone in the next town, we pick up the phone because we can't shout loudly enough for them to hear; and when we feel bored, we turn on the TV because it's easier than entertaining ourselves.

Services also enable us to achieve more in our relationships and careers, by expanding our minds, creating wealth, and organizing and even extending our lives. They can be emotionally laden; our relationships with doctors, dentists, faith leaders, lawyers, schools, even hairdressers, can span generations. In fact, most of the traditional rites of passage, from birth, through education, marriage, and finally to death, are facilitated by services.

Many of the services we use today are accessible through many channels, which adds an extra layer of complexity. We interact with organizations through websites and apps and in stores, over the phone with a human or a robot, in our own home, and while we're out and about. There are few moments in our day that aren't touched by services in some way.

You can see from this that getting services right can be a big deal, so it's worth designing them well. That's what great service design does. This book is about how to motivate and mobilize your people and teams to imagine, design and deploy better services that your customers will love and get them to market faster.

But why? Doing a better job for your customers feels intuitively like the right thing to do, yet making the case can feel like hard work. Investing in the experience for customers is seen by some in your organization as simply a cost, and therefore only worth doing if your customer satisfaction scores are taking a nose dive and your complaints are up. However, there is more to improving the design of services and the experience than placating aggrieved customers. For many organizations, customer experience design and management is the most important driver for growth in their industry. Why is this? Principally because they've done everything else. Those businesses that can now call themselves truly customer-centred either began that way or have spent a considerable amount of time over several years fixing their processes and changing their culture. They have organized themselves around their customers and this gives them a significant advantage, particularly for those in sectors that are commoditized, saturated, intermediated or where there are low barriers to switching. Where consumers see little difference between competitors on price and product quality, service drives the purchase decision and loyalty.

Improving the service you offer doesn't automatically mean increasing your operating costs. In fact, it can save you money in several important ways. Deploying technology to help keep track of your customers' orders and enquiries improves the service to them and reduces the human resources required. Designing a better experience for when things go wrong can help reduce the negative impact on your customers and retain some of their goodwill, which means you'll need to spend less to compensate and retain them. And most importantly, a design-led approach always helps you to spot ways to do more with less. In services this can mean, for example, developing a fantastic self-service proposition and experience that your customers love to use. Also, working with your colleagues and customers to redesign parts of your service can help reduce the number of errors made and avoid costly reworking or calls to your contact centre.

In addition to all these commercial benefits, running design-led projects with your teams in the ways we describe in this book can help transform your organization to be more customer-centred; to get better at designing and delivering for your customers. Working in this way will help your organization to see the service and experience you deliver as something they can consciously improve to impact commercial objectives. Teams will get closer to your customers and in doing so spot opportunities to make things easier and more enjoyable for them and find new solutions and propositions that keep them coming back. They'll be motivated to make change happen because the vision will excite them and feel like the right thing to be doing; the case and the plan will be clear. They'll feel they have permission to challenge, to use their imaginations and to experiment.

Before we go on we should define some terms:

- What is design?
- What is design-led change?
- What is customer experience?
- What makes a service?

What is design?

As trained designers we always try to avoid this very question at the risk of getting drawn into an argument over semantics. However, for the purposes of this book there are two important ideas to hold on to:

1 Design is about more than how things look.
   For us, the purpose of Design (with a capital 'D') is simply to tangibly improve things, to imagine and help realize solutions to real-world problems. They don't have to be huge and wicked problems (although they could be). They can be small but nevertheless important problems, for example, 'How do we reduce the number of customers closing their accounts after receiving their first bill from us?' or 'How do we get more young people to care about saving for their retirement?' or 'How do we make it easier to buy our products?'. Although we have trained as Designers (again, with a capital 'D') and we believe we have important skills and experience to offer, we also see ourselves as part of our clients' teams. Designing and delivering great services is very much a team effort.

And this brings us to the second important idea about Design:

2 Design is a process, not just a product, and it's a great process.
   There are many books written about the design process but, in essence, the design process starts with insight and ideas and works towards solutions. This doesn't sound revolutionary but historically many approaches to improvement and change in organizations have begun with the definition of the solution, with an individual or team writing a document that sets out the answer. However, as life has accelerated, systems have

become interlinked and more complex and the needs of consumers have diversified, it has become next to impossible to work in this way. As an alternative, the design process allows for exploration, experimentation and for the creativity of many to be applied to a problem or opportunity. The point at which the solution is fully defined is deferred for as long as is acceptable and, if possible, the solution is never fully defined but continually evolves in response to feedback from the people who use it.

So, when we use the term 'design' in this book we're referring to an approach to improving things that is well matched to the needs of organizations today. It's routed in customer insight. It's fuelled by ideas. It gives just enough structure to creativity and experimentation and, importantly, it's accessible, which means it's a great way to bring diverse expertise and experiences together, not just for a 'workshop' but to work through a process together.

What is design-led change?

When we use the term 'design-led change' we're suggesting there are two important outcomes for organizations. Firstly, to realize a better solution (product, service or experience) with benefits for customers and the business. And secondly, that the activities of designing also change the organization; the ways it organizes and operates. The premise for this book is our observation that once we've worked with an organization to redesign a service or improve the experience for its customers, there is no going back. That organization needs to make changes to their service operation and to their approach to service development and managing the experience for customers. Our conclusion: if you want to redesign your service and the experience your customers have, you often need to 'redesign' the people who'll design, implement and deliver those new solutions.

What is customer experience?

One route to answering this question is to think about the difference between 'customer service' and 'the customer experience'. When you have a picture of a service in your mind, it's normal to think of a help desk or a retail environment, but this is only part of the whole. Customer service tends to relate only to the contact a customer has with a company's people, and is usually restricted to transactions or queries. Customer experience, on the other hand, encompasses the holistic experience customers will have of a service. If you order a product online, for instance, your experience as a customer will start with a search or the advertisement you clicked, the process of choosing and buying your item, the follow-up information you were sent, tracking and waiting for the delivery, calls or chats with the contact centre if it didn't arrive, and unpacking the item and disposing of the packaging. The customer service elements of that experience were when you bought your item and had to contact them about the delivery issue; all the other aspects, including those, made up your overall experience.

The 'customer experience' is the sum of each and every experience your customers have of your products and services and, as a result, what they come to believe about your brand. Take a look at what we call the *Total Customer Experience Palette* in Table 0.1. You'll have spotted that *Customer Service* is just one of the headings and one aspect of the total customer experience (as we like to define it). Customers experience the combination of each of these aspects; they combine to form a perception of your business that drives their purchase decision.

Under each section of the Palette we've suggested some qualities or principles you could apply to the services you operate to define the total experience for your customers. Where is your focus and where are your strengths today?

The difficulty arises because control of each of these aspects often sits with different parts of a business. And when a business becomes large this combined impression becomes fragmented and the overall effect starts to unravel. The different ways that different functions of an organization interpret 'the customer experience', its relevance and their role in it can drive this sense of inconsistency and disjointedness that customers end up perceiving. Let's illustrate this with two examples.

In most organizations, customer service is the focus for Customer Operations teams. It's about managing inbound enquiries from customers and resolving their issues, and this is done mostly by people and increasingly by artificially intelligent systems. Particularly for organizations that sell clearly demarked products, whether manufactured in factories or, for example, financial products, 'customer service' and 'customer experience' have historically been synonymous. Product features and benefits are seen as the principal drivers of growth and product support a 'necessary evil'. Other parts of these businesses may not have seen themselves as having much of a role to play when it came to engendering the right perception in the minds of customers.

Equally, organizations whose products are less tangible, for example, mobile phone operators, tend to be marketing-led in their approach. They invest in their brand and in advertising to connect emotionally with consumers when product benefits are indistinct or hard to grasp. In many of these businesses the focus is 'customer value proposition' and service is promoted as a point of difference for the brand. However, in reality the service customers actually receive may not match the expectations set by the marketing.

So designing and delivering a great service and experience isn't just a challenge of imagination; it's an organizational challenge. Each area of the business needs to play its part. However, organizations often don't work like this and they aren't organized or skilled to work together on the 'total experience'.

In Table 0.1 we've suggested which functions within a business tend to adopt each aspect of the total experience as their own. In our experience, when a CEO sets a focus on the customer, and budgets follow, each area of the business will seek to 'own' the customer and the customer experience and adopt some aspect of the service and experience as their focus. However, the CEO's direction often isn't followed up with changes in approach, permission to work differently, incentives and skills. The result can feel like each part of the business is competing for ownership rather than collaborating to deliver the best possible total experience.

Great customer experience is no accident

So, which businesses manage to do all of this well and, importantly, bring it all together well? This is a tricky question as we all like different brands, but let's take the British airline Virgin Atlantic as an example (see Table 0.2).

What makes a service?

So how do services come about, and what do we think about them? Sometimes they evolve naturally and other times they're planned, but whatever the cause, they're designed and operated by people for other people. They can work well and make life more enjoyable for us, or they can work badly and frustrate and annoy us. It's easy to recall the difficult experiences we've had, whereas a service that's great can make our day. We want services to be, as a minimum, fit for purpose, but we're also longing for them to delight us by responding to us as individuals and to give us experiences that are valuable and memorable.

Table 0.1 Your customer experience is the sum total of each and every element of your customers' interactions with your business

	Total Customer Experience Palette					
	Service Performance	**Service Usability**	**Customer Service**	**Emotional Fulfilment**	**Brand Presence**	**Product Benefits**
			Things your customers think about when they're evaluating their experience and re-checking their perception of your brand			
	Frequent Fast Accurate Reliable Clean	Findable Accessible Convenient Navigable Simple Easy	Available Approachable Polite Personal Empathetic Resolution Recovery	Useful Desirable Enjoyable Cultural Safe Secure Rewarding	Distinctive Affirming Aspirational Endearing Exciting Enduring	Relevant Clear Valuable Price Package
	Areas of a business that adopt aspects of the Total Experience as their focus and as their way to take ownership of the customer					
	• IT • Operations • Process Excellence people	• Product Managers • Digital design • Retail design • Legal and compliance people	• Customer operations • HR roles • IT • Process Excellence people	• Product Managers • Customer Experience people	• Brand people • Customer Experience people	• Strategic Marketing • Commercial people • Technologists

Table 0.2 No service is perfect and there are plenty of poor reviews to be found online. But as a business, the airline Virgin Atlantic has always really understood the difference between 'customer service', which is essential for any airline, and designing the 'total customer experience'

		Total Customer Experience Palette – Virgin Atlantic			
Service Performance	Service Usability	Customer Service	Emotional Fulfilment	Brand Presence	Product Benefits
• Ranked 33 out of 100 for overall service in 2017 • In the Top 20 safest airlines again in 2017	Virgin Atlantic was one of the first major airlines to introduce self-serve check-in at London's Heathrow Airport. This coincided with the launch of the Upper Class 'Limo to Lounge' proposition at Heathrow, which made it effortless for Upper Class passengers to drive up to the terminal from their pre-booked limo and pass directly through a dedicated security lane and on to the Upper Class lounge.	• Awarded best European airline for long-haul flights in 2017 and 2018	4th-best business lounge in 2016, which is testament to how Virgin Atlantic responded in ways only they could to the need business people have to feel pampered and rewarded by their employer.	7th business Superbrand. The Virgin Group and Virgin Atlantic brands have appeared in the UK CoolBrands survey several times in the last 10 years. They invest heavily in very well-produced advertising that expresses their fun and entertainingly provocative personality, often satirizing their own brand image while portraying the glamour of flying. They have a unique style.	It's not always clear how these are distinct from others and it's fair to say that other airlines have caught up with a standard of service set by Virgin Atlantic and other long-haul airlines in the 1980s and 1990s. Virgin have always been known for their people and for using designers to great effect to create bold and original passenger lounges and aircraft interiors. They innovated in other areas too, for example, using an area of their Upper Class cabin to provide massages to passengers.

SOURCES Skytrax World Airline Awards 2017; The Airlines Ratings website; UK Superbrands Survey, 2017; UK Coolbrands Survey, 2001–2017

When we experience a service from the outside, we rarely consider all the moving parts that go into making it happen. But you'll know from the work you've done on the services you offer that a service is made up of a series of complex and interdependent systems. Each one has its own rules and structures, which must work together like a well-oiled engine in order for them to operate effectively. This can involve your organization changing not only *what* it delivers to your customers, but also *how* it delivers it.

Figure 0.1   Services are working systems of people and technologies designed to create value for businesses and their customers

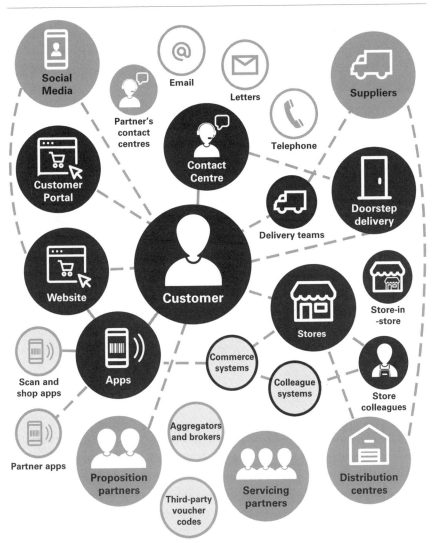

It's not as easy as it looks

As we know, creating and delivering the services our customers want isn't easy. We interact with human beings so often through the services we use, it's surprising how often they lack empathy and humanity. The cliché of the customer service operative robbed of autonomy by 'the system' is stubbornly clinging on, albeit with a loosening grip. This is because it can be as hard for those providing a service to engage with the diversity of their customers as it is for those same customers to accept the limitations of the complex system those providers work with and the industry models they operate within.

So why do people in organizations find it so hard to develop great services that not only work, but resonate with their customers? There are three main reasons:

- They have the desire to provide an amazing service, but there's an imagination gap between this desire and envisioning what it would look like in reality.

- They have a vision, but the change needed to deliver it feels too big and scary.

- They don't have the right skills and capabilities to create the service, so although it may function, it will never delight their customers.

If you work in a job that requires you to develop and manage services for your customers, you'll probably have experienced first-hand the complexity of this situation. Which way do you go? What do you do first? How do you cut through the difficulty of designing and implementing services that will bring your customers back again and again? This doesn't just relate to those who have direct contact with your customers, by the way, but to everyone in your business who has an influence on the customer experience as a whole.

There are three different levels you could be at right now:

1 Fix: Your service is broken and you need to fix it. You're getting poor customer satisfaction scores and there's no option but to do something about it, and quickly.

2 Develop: You want to develop your services so your customers have a better experience of them, or move your service proposition on a step. Maybe you've seen your competitors doing things better, or there could have been a significant change in your business that means you need to restructure your service offering. Alternatively, it could simply be that you have an ongoing process of improving the performance of your business.

3 Transform: You're on a mission to transform your services, making significant changes to what you're doing and how you're doing it. Perhaps you're new to your role (or your manager is) and you want to put a rocket up your service delivery. Or maybe a new, cross-functional customer experience team has been formed, triggering an investigation in this area. Whatever the trigger, transforming your services in this way will require you to transform your organization too.

Wherever you're at, you've probably been tasked with giving your customers what they love. But this raises questions: who are your customers? What services would they be delighted by? And – the big one – how will you convince your colleagues to work with you to create and deliver them? You know picking around the edges of the problem is unlikely to be the answer, because you've tried that before. And continuing to fix problems only as they arise doesn't feel like the solution and might even be a waste of resources if those small improvements are undermined by larger issues. No – you want to create a comprehensive vision for the design of your service in your organization, and then make it a reality.

To achieve this, it helps to have a visionary imagination, deep insight into your customers' minds, and commitment to the cause. You'll also find it essential to develop a keen sense of connection with your customers' emotions, and a way of crafting quality services that are elegant and work beautifully.

Sounds like a tall order, doesn't it? Don't worry, that's where this book comes in. As partners and designers at Engine Service Design (one of the first service design consultancies in the world), we've been helping $1 billion-plus organizations reshape and re-imagine their services for over 18 years. In that time, we've learned a lot about how to design and make things happen in complex organizations – and why things fail, too.

Just as it might be in your own company, many of our clients have gained their commercial advantage through a combination of increased marketing spend, operational efficiency and digital transformation. The problem is, they now recognize the limits of pursuing efficiency and technology alone. This means that as more becomes possible, the age-old questions become more crucial: what will our customers value most, what will make them buy from us, and how do we get more of the right services to market faster? To rise to these challenges requires us to embrace a different mindset and approach, not just to design and development, but to the business change needed to create and deliver new products and services.

Being design-led

So, what makes some organizations better at doing this than others? The successful ones are moving from a management approach that's technology, marketing or resource optimization-led, to one that's customer-inspired and vision-led with a more experimental and speedy pace. This is a management approach that engages and excites teams, and recognizes that the right order in which to do things is to use customer insight to inform the service proposition, to design the customer experience from that, and finally to develop the capabilities needed to deliver it.

Approaching the challenges of improvement and change in a way that is 'design-led' recognizes that putting something new and of value in customers' hands isn't just about completing a product development cycle. It's also about inspiring and supporting an organization to invest in it, implement it well, and sell and support it brilliantly.

Our experience points to seven design-led competencies that help organizations get the right services to market faster:

- Creating a compelling vision that leads to a purposeful service design.
- Crafting a beautiful service design that 'just works'.
- Making a clear case for why it's important so everyone can buy into it.
- Ensuring it's ready to build, so there are no mistakes when it's implemented.
- Creating the right conditions for it to be put into place quickly and efficiently.
- Making sure the project is engaging and fun, so everyone wants to be a part of it.
- Focusing on the quality throughout the process, so what's created for customers is of a high quality too.

This isn't an approach we've developed overnight; in fact we've created it by working shoulder to shoulder with our clients over the years. Often we learned by being asked to do new things and to answer challenging questions that nobody had considered before. For example, we saw how difficult our clients found it to decide which parts of their vision or design to take forward. Making judgements about things that don't exist yet can be tricky, and the process seemed subjective and often driven by personalities, rather than how to create maximum value. So we created a way of assessing our proposals that we could run as collaborative workshops; these worked well at removing the barriers to value-based decision-making. Now we run these workshops whenever we do a project.

We've also discovered the only way of creating an ambitious vision of what your customers will want in the future, as well as today, is to take an 'outside-in' approach. If you start from the viewpoint of what you already have, rather than putting yourself in your customers' shoes and working out what it is they truly desire, you're limiting yourself. To win over and impress your customers requires empathy and understanding.

We never forget, though, that a marvellous idea is only as good as the system that can make it work. There's a kind of dance you have to do between imagining a service, and building a service design that can actually happen within the operating environment of your company. Also, getting the balance right between the big picture and the small detail can be key.

This book will help you do all these things. And, although we work with many large businesses, some of the projects we've led have been on a limited area of their operations, so our approach is completely scalable. It's not just for complete transformations either; it will help you improve on and innovate with a service you provide already. Through the results we get, we've proved that the same approaches, tools, mindset and ways of thinking can apply equally to any size or scale of organization, whatever the ambition of their change.

We've split the book into two parts. The first addresses the six main challenges you'll already be facing when it comes to creating the services your customers will love. There's enormous value and comfort in understanding what these are, because without knowing where you're currently at, you won't be able to move forward. The second part takes you through the seven competencies you'll need if you're to become a design-led service organization. By the end of this, you'll understand the approaches and mindset required to be in the top tier of service businesses. Let's now briefly introduce both the challenges and the competencies.

The challenges

The first challenge and the first chapter of the book identifies what is surely the first step in designing a great service, and indeed towards becoming a more customer-centred organization: developing the organizational capability to see the world through your customers' eyes. Although obvious it's not easy, yet understanding them and, more powerfully, being inspired by them and their worlds will significantly impact how you work and the products, services and experiences you put out there in the market.

Chapter 2 is all about the importance of vision. Even in organizations that have developed more agile ways of making changes and delivering new products, emotional and financial investment in more significant changes over a longer period requires a bigger idea. The challenge is that the word 'vision' is ambiguous; everybody seems to have one and the whole thing can grind to a halt because key people in your organization simply can't imagine what the vision means in reality.

Chapter 3 explores the healthy and important tension that exists across organizations between the need to get things done and the need to plan ahead, the need to respond to changing requirements in the moment and to prepare for the near or more distant future. This tension manifests itself when teams get together to collaborate. It manifests itself in the sometimes-conflicting objectives set by departments and functions and in the personalities of key people in the organization. The opportunity is to accept that this tension exists, that both 'metabolic rates' and responses are needed, and to find the design tools and methods that ensure both can be managed together.

Chapter 4 explores one of the important drivers for commercial success in many of the sectors in which we work – emotion. There are many factors essential for operating a successful business model but it's increasingly the case that differentiation in your market stems from an ability to connect on the level of emotions with your customers – to recognize that your customers are emotional beings. In addition, of course, emotion counts inside your organization too and particularly when it comes to the challenge of changing your organization to improve the service and experience for your customers. The problem is that although we all have emotions and these drive our decisions as consumers and employees, businesses can sometimes operate as though we don't.

Chapter 5 explores another important aspect of design that shapes consumers' choices and your customers' perception of your business: the extent to which the service you offer and the experience your customers have feels 'distinct' from your competitors. If product and price are on a par with the competition and the basics of customer service are working as they should, then what's that 10 per cent that ensures your customers want a Virgin Atlantic experience over a British Airways or American Airlines experience? And how is this difference realized beyond the visual branding, uniforms and aircraft livery?

Chapter 6 identifies the central challenge, the challenge of making things happen. You may have the vision and great design for a service. You may have figured out how to make it all work and make it feel distinctly your brand. Yet, your project is vulnerable. Senior colleagues might lack the imagination, or the climate makes the changes feel too risky and your peers are focused elsewhere with shorter-term objectives to deliver. There will always be reasons not to do something, so how do you equip yourself with the understanding, ideas and tools to get more of the right things to market?

The skills

In Chapter 7 we set out the importance of having an actionable vision for your service and how to make it a compelling one. We propose a way to understand and to communicate to others what a vision really is and its true purpose, and we explore some of the elements to consider if you want to ensure that your vision is both compelling and complete.

Chapter 8 is about beauty. This may seem like an odd topic for a business management title but bear with us. In this chapter we discuss the notion that services and experiences can be 'well crafted' and indeed 'beautiful' and we put some parameters around what this means in practice. Importantly, beauty is of course more than skin deep. For us the word beauty is short-hand for a service design that's a pleasure to use not only because all the touchpoints with the service look great but because they also work well. In fact, all parts of the service work well together – the underlying proposition is genuinely valuable to me and the whole thing feels fit for purpose. More fundamentally, the service I'm using and the brand it represents somehow feel right for me and for the time and culture in which I'm living. And on top of that, there is a twist of originality that draws me in and keeps me coming back for more. Getting all this right is surely beautiful service design?

Chapter 9 provides us with a dose of pragmatism and suggests that even with the most compelling vision and the most beautifully designed solutions, any business worth its success will need to be great at making the case internally to move forward. The problem is that all too often businesses assess options and construct business cases based on cost and predictions about performance using historical data. They also use the defence of short-term objectives and the need to fix the basics to limit the appeal of projects that will really make a difference in the market. So, how can you construct a clear case when there is no data with which to predict performance because the solution is too new?

Chapter 10 responds to the reality that making new services and experiences happen, large or small, requires that many people and teams do their part, often including delivery partners and suppliers. This presents a risk. In Part One we identified the challenge of translating a vision into a solution and into action across teams. So, how do you ensure that that vision isn't, well, lost in translation?

Chapter 11 explores the importance of creating and sustaining the right conditions within your organization for your project to progress and succeed. We suggest some of the ways that design methods, storytelling and continuing to make your customers somehow present throughout your project can help maintain focus and momentum.

Chapter 12 faces up to the reality that people are busy. You are busy and so are the people whose help you need. All the organizations we've worked with have far too much to do and your project can just feel like yet another thing. So how can you make your project the one people want to work on? In this chapter we delve a little deeper, describing some practical ways to draw people and resources towards you and keep your team interested and excited about what you're doing.

Chapter 13 reflects on the specific skills and mindset of trained Designers and our practice at Engine Service Design. Yes, it's a sales pitch for a specific set of skills but we also point out approaches and some of the habits of Designers you can adopt in your role. Although you may not feel like a Designer right now, you're probably already thinking like one and if there are core skills that you lack (such as visualization skills), there may be others in your organization that have them.

Throughout this book you'll discover how to model different ways of working that you can transfer to other parts of your business, and all your future roles. We don't believe in learning something that only works in one area of a business or in one sector, and which you can't replicate because you don't understand the principles behind it. Instead, we'll be showing you how, by getting your head around the principles of being 'design-led', you can take this knowledge into every project you work on – much to your company's benefit (and therefore your own).

Getting your organization's services working successfully for both your business and your customers isn't an option, it's a fundamental necessity. There are numerous challenges and opportunities involved in doing this, but if you get it right you have the potential to turn your business into the one everyone wants to buy from. There's no time to lose, though. As a consumer yourself, you'll know how impatient you are for the ideal customer experience and your own customers are no different. Designing, planning and implementing great services has never been so important.

PART ONE
The challenges

We know creating and delivering an inspirational customer experience can be hard. If it wasn't, every business would be doing it effortlessly and we'd all be delighted by services every day. So what are the challenges we all face in giving our customers the services that make them want to come back for more? There are six of them, and Part One goes through them in detail.

Although it may seem as if we're only focusing on the negatives here, this part of the book is designed to make you feel better. Your problems are almost certainly similar to those faced by managers in other service-based organizations. The difference between you and them, though, is that by the end of Part One you'll understand the issues so much better than they will, and will therefore be primed to tackle them through the skills in Part Two.

Developing the ability to spot and articulate these challenges is the first step towards being able to share them with your colleagues. As you become better at designing great services, you'll be glad you took the time to understand the challenges first.

The challenge of outside-in 01

Cast your mind back to the last time you called your phone or utilities provider. Most likely you had to make a selection from a bewildering and increasingly intricate series of menu options before you finally got through to a human being, at which point you were asked to repeat the security details you'd already entered at the beginning. You may have been tempted to vent your frustration, but after taking a deep breath the knot in your stomach began to subside. 'It's not the customer service agent's fault,' you reminded yourself, 'it's the system they work with.'

It's not much better when we wait in for an important online order delivery, only to find it doesn't arrive. All we have from the delivery provider is an email with the expected time on it – there's no way of contacting them to ask when it's going to turn up. Or if there is, it's a link to their tracking tool, which simply says the delivery 'has left our depot'. How helpful. Increasingly frustrated, we log on to the website from which we ordered the item and call their customer service team. At which point, cue a repeat of the scenario above.

Thankfully these scenarios are becoming less common. Day-to-day transactions at least take place quickly and easily, often via our smartphones. More joined-up and intelligent systems are taking more of the effort out of our basic requests. Yet, paradoxically, we often have the worst experiences when we need real help and understanding the most; when we no longer fit the standard business process, when we need a human and a machine won't quite cut it.

Why do customers still have difficult, impersonal, maddening and, in the worst of cases, antagonistic interactions with the services they use? The main reason this happens is that many companies don't organize themselves around the customer and their experience. Without this customer-centredness, companies miss out on its commercial benefits, and they also risk wasted time and effort.

In this chapter we identify some of the common mistakes and lost opportunities for businesses that are not customer-centred. For example, without understanding what your customers need and will value most there's a risk that you spend time launching the wrong products and services. Without a shared customer strategy, there's a risk of duplication of effort as different departments set to work tackling what they see the problems to be. Without a shared vision and plan, departments can even find themselves pulling in opposite directions. Work started with the best of intentions ends up perpetuating a service experience that's not coherent or joined up.

One important barrier to being customer-centred and working outside-in is the 'siloed' structure of many organizations. Although necessary in some respects, this structural barrier seems to prevent large organizations from doing two important things: seeing the world as their customers see it (rather than through the objectives of a business function and professional skill set) and seeing their own services as customers experience them (as a whole and joined up). The management challenge is to work horizontally (opening up the possibility of greater customer focus) and vertically (maintaining the core functions of the business and delivery) at the same time.

We've worked with organizations to understand and assess how customer-centred they are; how able they are to put the customer, metaphorically, at the centre of design and decision-making. To do this you first must have viewed the world and your brand and services through their eyes; in other words, from the outside in.

Opportunities missed by businesses that are not customer-centred

Let's explore what happens when the services you provide don't take your customers' perspectives as their starting point. The consequences fall into four main areas, and they're not necessarily the ones you would predict.

You might waste time and money launching a service your customers don't want or need

Surely no-one does this, do they? Unfortunately, they do. It usually happens because the company is working with the wrong assumptions about what its customers value. Without clear insight and a process in place to imagine and test assumptions and ideas, the new service development will tend to be ad hoc, and occasionally even subject to the whims of individual decision-makers who don't understand all the implications. Something that seems like a bright, shiny idea in theory doesn't always work in practice, because not enough thought has been put into whether people value it, or how they might use it.

As an example, in 2013 Facebook launched Facebook Home, an optional home screen Android for smartphones, which showed the owner's Facebook newsfeed. The problem was, most people didn't like having no control over the content displayed on their home screen, which meant it was only appealing to Facebook obsessives. This, together with the high data and battery usage involved, and the fact that it was a paid subscription service, led to its downfall (Baer and Yarrow, 2014).

Crispin from the Rail Delivery Group highlights the reality that organizations often make decisions based on assumptions about their customers:

> Very often organizations have never asked their teams to put their feet in the shoes of the customer. Decisions are made based upon assumptions about what the customer wants, upon business need or upon a mixture of both. It should come as no surprise that when asked to do so, organizations can struggle. When the Rail Delivery Group established the Customer Directorate in 2015, it did so using existing teams and very few had ever been asked to think about the customer; in fact, only a very small percentage of the team mentioned the word customer when describing their role. It took time to change that – it was a complete change in thinking.

It's the easiest thing in the world to make mistaken assumptions about what services your customers want to buy, and not as difficult as you might think to find out for real. We'll be exploring how you do this throughout the book but the best approach is simply to spend some time with them.

You can create or perpetuate dysfunctional processes

Many companies view service as operating a set of customer processes, rather than as a holistic experience. As a customer yourself, how often have you had to fill out overly detailed forms or provide the same information several times, in order to support a set of disjointed processes? This happens because those organizations haven't stepped into their customers' worlds and understood what interacting with them is like. Instead, they expect their customers to compensate for their own poor process design. Organizations within the charity sector, for example, often have come to expect people to donate, and have become reliant on low-cost, high-volume direct marketing. It's important these players face up to a 'new reality' and understand the current pressures from regulators to tone down what is now considered to be aggressive canvassing for donations. Instead, they can adopt an outside-in mindset and focus on how their support customers want to be treated and engaged with.

Your efforts might get duplicated

Until relatively recently, it wasn't uncommon for several different departments in a large company to operate their own customer website for their particular sales or servicing area; there was no coherent view of the customer experience or of the duplication inside the business. The result was a mushrooming of the number of websites over time, each requiring their own customer login and providing a disjointed and often frustrating experience for their customers (to say nothing of a poor impression of the brand).

We often audit the communications that businesses send to customers at points in the service journey and when we do it almost always comes as a surprise how many there are and, more importantly, how inconsistent they are. Each function involved in delivering the service communicates slightly differently. Organizations with many products and many teams often end up bombarding their customers with duplicated or conflicting sales messages.

You might see your customers as a burden, rather than as inspiration for your future competitive advantage

It's unusual to return a faulty product and receive a completely helpful and positive response. Customers are still asked to 'justify their case' by returning the goods (at their cost and inconvenience) or arguing their point. The assumption from most businesses seems to be that customers are 'trying it on' unless the purchaser can prove otherwise. For organizations that don't need to make a sale or profit directly from their end customer, for example, those in the public sector or monopoly privately owned (but regulated) public infrastructure, customer service and a consideration of the customer experience as a whole is often a conversation about controlling cost or spending only to appease customers who might otherwise do nothing but complain.

This outlook is improving, mainly due to the readiness of customers to complain on social media if they feel they've had a raw deal. Many companies would now rather agree to rework, refund or exchange than have a public fight with their customers about it. They've seen the cost of returns is relatively small, but the impact of bad press is huge. It's also time-consuming to pursue a drawn-out argument at the till, when there's a queue of customers waiting to hand over their cash. Most people are honest, after all, so why not trust them? What's more, if this mindset shift is handled well in an organization, it can even lead to a change in the way the whole business thinks about its customers. If it believes the world is full of dishonest people, this shapes its culture, guides decisions about the design of its service, and affects the way it communicates. On the other hand, if its view is more optimistic it will project a more caring image.

Of course, the trusting approach isn't always as simple as it sounds. Take the insurance sector, for example, which a minority of people do try to defraud. Understandably, its culture has always been based on managing risk, and as a result it doesn't have the greatest reputation for customer experience. However, insurers have begun to think of themselves not as companies selling financial products, but as people who connect with key events in their customers' lives. We all take out insurance for emotional reasons – to protect our home, our health, or our financial security – and the businesses that have made the greatest progress have been those that have re-engineered their services, and re-trained their staff, to connect emotionally with their policy holders. They do their due diligence, but in a way that recognizes the emotional impact of the situation their customer is in.

Imagine a financial services company that sells life and critical illness insurance. It has always believed that its purpose was to sell policies and process claims. When challenged by the CEO to 'improve the service to customers', teams set about re-engineering the sales and claims processes, removing waste and slowly converting paper into online forms. They saw some successes, but they were still getting complaints and were not where they wanted to be in the league tables for their industry.

Somebody suggested that they speak to their customers and when they did they learned a lot. They realized that what they saw as 'the customer journey' was not what customers experienced – it wasn't their journey. Their customers were dealing with either a bereavement or the diagnosis of a severe or life-threatening illness. The impact of these events on their customers' lives and how much they had to deal with suddenly became clear.

Today, when their customers make a claim, agents ask them a series of supportive questions designed to help them work through their situation, and can guide their 'members' (no longer 'claimants') to other services beyond their own if that's what's most helpful. The company realized that it's not just what the service does, it's how it makes people feel that counts. And this shift in perspective and approach returned significant commercial benefits.

If you've been thinking carefully about some of the things that can go wrong when a company doesn't organize itself around its customers, you may have realized that they all have one thing in common. They're the result of the vertical silos that typify the structure of many large organizations. Inherent in this is the difficulty of getting all the parts of the business to work cooperatively with each other, and to organize themselves around the needs of customers. When there's an interdependence between one silo and another, this is where customers can fall through the gaps.

Let's take a closer look at how silos are responsible for this problem (and don't worry if this seems unsurmountable; we'll suggest solutions later).

The effect of your silos on your customers

When a business gets to a certain size it's organized by department. It has to be, otherwise the functions of the business, such as marketing, IT, buying and finance, can't run effectively. But this causes a problem for customers, because decisions that affect the service they receive are not based on a holistic view of what's best for them, but on what's easiest for the structure, leadership and management of each business area. So, using our utility company example from before, the sales team might have the aim of retaining customers who are thinking of leaving, but they're not so interested in solving the problems that have caused them to leave in the first place. Nor does the person running field operations always think to ask the people in the contact centre whether and why customers call up following a visit from one of their engineers. That's someone else's job. The customer, of course, doesn't care about the individual departments in the company – they just want great service. So how do you get around this?

When we work with organizations to help them re-engineer their customers' experiences, we help them create a 'horizontal practice', which is totally focused on their customers. This cuts across the company structure without disturbing what already exists, and is the most efficient way of bringing the customer experience into the company consciousness. In a way, we're creating (or building on) another well-established horizontal function like HR or IT support, allowing these businesses to organize themselves around their customers in a way they may have never done before.

We worked in this way for a major retailer in the UK over two years. As you'd expect, it has many physical stores as well as its online store, and it knew its consumers expected the experience they had with it to have a similar set of qualities whether they shopped online, using the app, or by going into a store. If you'd paid a visit to its headquarters, however, you'd have seen that it wasn't organized around its customers. Like all similar-sized businesses, it operated in silos, with a marketing department, customer operations, product teams, a digital technology department and so on. In fact, it had several businesses all operating under one brand, all contributing to the customer experience but not seeing it as a whole. As a response to this, it created a team to re-examine the entire customer experience, and our role was to develop a set of ideas and tools for that team that would help them build bridges across these silos. Eventually, responsibility for customer experience no longer sat within one team, but became an organizing principle for the business. This move was supported by an intranet dedicated to communicating internally their understanding of who their customers are and the practices of customer experience design.

Once companies reach a certain size and complexity they have to organize into departments of specialists. But by creating the right governance, establishing the right projects and cross-functional teams, you can make a temporary bridge without a wholesale restructure.

Where we've got this working well the organization has moved beyond the structure of a single Customer Experience team sitting in one department or another. Instead, customer experience management has become a cross-business function with a network of CX Managers operating as business partners supported by a toolkit and training resources. The creation of a *Customer Experience Network* focuses the organization on skills rather than roles and responsibilities as supportive of the reality that service is the product of the whole organization and delivering a great total customer experience is the challenge for the whole organization.

Failure to balance the tension between the commercial model and providing an amazing experience

Most businesses exist to make a profit, and in order to do this they must (among other things) delight their customers so they come back again and again. However, there is often a tension between the commercial model and providing an amazing experience. The best companies make sure they're balancing the need to make money in the short term, with a focus on their customers as living, breathing individuals who want a brilliant experience right now. The customer experience becomes an absolute imperative for businesses in markets focused on retention; it's easier to sell to an existing customer than to acquire a new one.

A customer-centric organization is one with a shared direction, values and behaviours. It can focus everybody on improving the experience for customers. It's the ability and readiness of companies to adopt this outside-in approach that makes or breaks their customers' experiences. However, being a perfectly customer-centred organization able to stand in its customers' shoes and respond continuously with creativity and agility isn't easy. No organization we've ever worked with gets it right all the time. In fact, to be a success in the market you operate in, you probably don't need to be great at everything. The important steps are to understand the capabilities that are important for your business in your sector and marketplace and to focus there.

We worked with the European energy group E.ON over several years and in four of their European markets. As part of our work with the Group Customer Experience Team we developed a customer-centricity maturity model. This framework was deployed across the organization as a survey to gauge maturity and more importantly to grow awareness that being customer-centred was the responsibility of all parts of the business.

The customer-centricity framework contains 111 organizational functions that contribute to customer-centeredness. These are grouped into six broad areas:

- Strategic direction and commitment: Do you know what you stand for, where you're going, and what it will take for each employee to get you there?

- Culture and management: Do you have the structure and culture to get you to where you want to be?

- Delivery enablement: Is your whole business lined up behind your frontline so you can deliver for your customers?

- An understanding of your customers and their worlds: Does your whole business understand your customers?

- Experience in design and development: Can you rapidly change your services to respond to your customers' changing needs?

- Delivery quality and assurance: Do you deliver experiences that meet your customers' needs?

You can see how hard it can be to achieve anything close to perfection, especially when you consider the cross-functional and multichannel nature of the challenge, with each of your customer touchpoints and back-office teams playing their part in design and delivery. Technology is part of the solution, but it's also necessary to align and enable people, environments, processes and communications. Being skilled in working across teams and functions is important. 'Joining the dots' internally makes it easier to join the dots for your customers.

The business units within the E.ON Group that used the survey were able to share their scores with their teams and also compare their scores with other markets. Generating the scores was interesting and got people talking about the model, but more importantly teams could diagnose why they were where they were and what they could do about it.

So no, it's not easy, and it never was. But moving towards being able to see each of your customers as one real, living person, not as separate facets of the same person depending on who they interact with in your business, is an exciting challenge.

Key takeaways

- If your business isn't organized around managing your customers' experience, you're almost certainly frustrating and annoying them in some way or another. Elements of this you'll already know about, but many you won't.

- Spending time with your customers is the most fruitful way of discovering the reality of the journey, and their relationship with your business, through their eyes. To them, it may look and feel radically different from how you assume it is. They may want and expect things you're not delivering, or appreciate elements of your offering you'd ignored or taken for granted.

- There are several pitfalls for any business that's not customer-centred, including:

  - If you don't understand what your customers most value, you risk launching services they don't want or need. This wastes time and money that could have been spent delighting instead of disappointing them.

  - When your business isn't joined up in its service delivery across all departments, it will create dysfunctional and repetitive processes that don't take your customers' desires into account. Just because each function is doing what it thinks is best, it doesn't mean the experience is working for your customers.

  - You're likely to overlook the elements of your service your customers genuinely value, because you don't know what they want in the first place. At best this can lead to you not maximizing their benefits, and at worst can lead to you accidentally jettisoning something that makes your brand appealing.

- When different departments see different customer service elements as important, they pull in different directions and this creates inconsistency in service delivery. That's why, as consumers ourselves, we can have a great experience of a bank's branch service, and a terrible one of its charging structure.

- A disjointed view of your customers across your business makes it more challenging to serve them well. Without a single view it's much harder to avoid unnecessary effort for the customer, confusion, duplication and missed opportunities to retain customers who are becoming dissatisfied.

● The majority of these pitfalls are caused by the existence of silos in organizations. All companies work in functional departments, and this is necessary for the smooth running of the business. But customers have a habit of falling through the gaps between the silos, because no single team has a focus on their overall experience, or the ability to see their services from the customer's perspective.

● The solution is to create an internal customer experience network in your business that is able to work across the silos, dedicated to understanding, managing and promoting the customer experience.

● All of this requires striking a balance between the need of your business to make a profit now, and to focus on delighting its customers in the short and long term. Perfection is impossible, but establishing and applying a shared vision and behaviours will help ensure the effort and resources invested result in outcomes that are greater than the sum of the parts.

Reference

Baer, D and Yarrow, J (2014) 22 of the most epic product fails in history, *Business Insider UK*, 31 July. Available online at: http://uk.businessinsider.com/biggest-product-failures-in-business-history-2014-7

The challenge of vision

02

Every great service starts with a vision. It might not be a conscious one. That faithful convenience store owner that always remembered your name and put aside the things she knew you always needed never wrote down a service vision but she may have had an intuitive sense of the role she wanted to play in her community, how she wanted to treat people and where she wanted to take her business. We'll be going into more detail about vision in Chapter 7, but for now it's enough to understand that an outstanding vision achieves an elegant marriage of a desired future for your business, a compelling proposition for your customers, and – just as importantly – a powerful motivator for your organization to change.

It's true that businesses can succeed without a vision. A strategy for growth, to increase volumes and efficiency will drive the bottom line. However, it's likely that at some point the current business model and product offering will stop being fit for its purpose or the market will change around you. At this point the ambition and purpose for the business may need to be reset. And a vision is about more than defining what success looks like (these are objectives); a vision is about emotion, motivation and excitement. There are many reasons to get yourself a compelling vision.

In this chapter we'll make the case for why businesses still need a clear vision if they want to make significant change happen and respond to major shifts in their operating environment. Despite the need for a vision, creating and using one can be tricky, not least because 'vision' is an ambiguous term, so the first task is to agree what a vision is and what you need it to do. And there are other pitfalls. Whose vision is it? What's the timeframe for achieving it? What should it… envision? What happens once you have one? We'll set out what we see as the big differences between the corporate objectives of a business and a vision for that business, and this is often where some confusion lies.

And, as you'll probably know, it's one thing having a great idea and another making it happen. For a start, framing the right vision isn't as easy as you might think, at whatever scale, and after that there are several obstacles you will have to overcome to make it real. It's this translation of vision as a concept into reality that many organizations struggle with. We'll identify some of the things that can go wrong.

Probably the greatest barrier to great visioning, though, is imagination; the ability to run ahead and construct an idea of what your future service or business will actually be like and pull these ideas back into the present so that other people imagine them too. We'll discuss the importance of finding a vision that is compelling, that feels aspirational enough but achievable – one that's able to motivate your teams, partners and ultimately your customers. We'll return to the subject of visions in Chapter 7 and look in more detail at how to construct what we often call a 'pragmatic aspiration' for your business.

Before we go much further though, we should probably set out what we see as the difference between a vision and a strategy. In a nutshell, your vision is a depiction of the business or service (or perhaps world) you want to create, and your strategy is how you're going to create it. Your strategy may contain several elements, including the roadmap for that development and details of the general approach and specific actions to take. You'll also set objectives that help to quantify the vision, steps along the way and when you've achieved it. Visions don't always have to be transformational or indeed... visionary. They can address an unglamourous business issue. But they should be far enough out of reach and, if achieved, in some way change the game for your business and customers.

Why you need a vision

Let's think first about why you need a vision of what you want your customer experience to look and feel like. In summary, all organizations need to make clear, reasoned decisions about limited resources. A vision brings structure to resource planning, decision-making and investment. From a funding point of view, it means you can have a meaningful conversation about budgets with your colleagues higher up the organization, with that money more likely to be spent in an efficient and coordinated way. It also helps everyone aim at the same destination, which makes planning easier. What's more, a vision helps set the scene and make your case for change, so it's motivating and exciting enough for all departments to put in the effort. Once people can see the business is moving forward as a result, everyone wants to make it work.

Equally, a vision is a useful tool for your board to manage their relationships with their senior stakeholders and shareholders. If questions are asked at your next shareholders' meeting about what your business is doing to anticipate changes in customers' expectations, your CEO is better able to present a credible response.

On the other hand, let's think about what happens when you don't have a vision. In this scenario people are liable to make ad hoc, incremental improvements, which in isolation may be too small to register with customers as new, exciting or valuable. Your colleagues are less likely to feel enthusiastic about the end goal, leaving your plans vulnerable to being dropped in favour of the next shiny new idea. And, most significantly, by fixing one small system over here, and plugging another gap over there, you'll find it harder to gain sign-off for a more transformational piece of work that would help you build something that works better for your customers.

So a vision doesn't just describe a future state, it has a broader role in implementing your plans. You can see now how vital it is to have an agreed vision.

Why is it so hard to translate a vision into reality?

The road between theory (a vision) and practice (a service both existing and being used) has many potholes, diversions, and – in more cases than you'd like to think – dead ends. Assuming your vision is sound, what could go wrong when translating it into reality? From working with countless organizations struggling with this process we've learned there are several causes:

- A lack of common understanding across the business about what a vision is.
- A lack of commitment to it because it's just not compelling enough.
- A misplaced belief that the articulation of a vision is the whole job done.
- A lack of appropriate timescales; either too short-term to appear distinct from what is already in the plan or too long-term to feel relevant or achievable.
- A lack of clarity about how to translate the vision into tangible change.
- A lack of agreement about whose responsibility it is to manifest the vision.

Luckily, a design-led approach provides some specific answers to these challenges, as we'll see in Part Two. For now, let's look at the difficulties in more detail. See which ones resonate with you.

Confusion about what a vision is

Unfortunately, many organizations think they have a customer experience vision, but they don't. That's because they don't fully understand, or agree upon, what a vision is and what it's for. Business-planning terms such as vision, strategy, mission and targets are highly interpretable and to some people interchangeable, so one team might think their company has a customer experience 'vision' while what they have is a set of commercial objectives or a set of statements describing how they'd like the company to be perceived by customers and their industry. It's the confusion around these terms that leads people to make different assumptions about what their business needs to achieve.

Let's imagine a fictional health insurer. We'll call them *Bermondsey Health Insurance International*. The company wants to create a future vision, and to achieve this, their senior executives lock themselves away in a series of meetings, which result in three statements and an action plan. Essentially these statements say: we want to make more money, attract more customers, and make sure we're a nice place to work. Table 2.1 is an illustration of the differences between each of the elements they came up with, which are often confused with a vision for the company, service or customer experience.

Table 2.1   Most companies seek focus through a collection of strategic statements, yet none of those below envision the service and customer experience needed to realize the objectives and benefits they define

Bermondsey Health Insurance International	
Objectives and targets	£500 k in new policies under risk by Q4 next year
Statement of intent or mission statements	Be the world's most trusted health insurer
Corporate strapline	'Working to make you well'
Action plan	Build customer culture programme Develop our partnership capability Grow our health provider network Rebrand Implement a global CRM solution

This fictional illustration shows that although each of these statements has its uses, none describe what the business is actually going to create for its customers and how doing so will realize the benefits described in the table.

Apart from the fact that many companies would strive for the same, these statements don't form a vision – they are simply statements of intent. 'We want to make more money' sounds like an aim, but it's actually a question. If they want to make more money, what do they need to do? What kind of company should they be? What services would they operate? How much should they spend on providing services compared to what they charge for them? They thought they had a vision but what they actually had was a set of objectives in search of a vision.

A vision would have presented answers to these questions, which is where design thinking comes in. 'Design thinking' is excellent at pulling the future backwards into the present so we can see it as if it were already here. It's a bit like a movie showing the future: three years from now our customers will be able to do 'this' and spend money with us in 'these' ways and, as a result, they'll understand us to be the business and brand we need them to see, which will mean we're able to achieve our commercial objectives.

Without imagining what the service should be and without being able to link these tangible concepts to the tangible benefits they're seeking, this fictional business will probably continue making incremental changes and improvements to its current service and business model. This may not get it to where it wants to be.

So to summarize, a vision is not:

- a set of objectives or targets;
- a statement of intent or mission statements;
- a new corporate strapline;
- an action plan.

In our experience, a vision has a clear role to play alongside the other elements in the table. A vision should:

- vividly and tangibly describe a future state in which your business is achieving its commercial objectives;
- be complete and well informed so your business can use it to make decisions (a lot of work is carried out to create visions that are then quietly dismissed as fanciful, unnecessary or unrealistic);
- be exciting and practical enough to motivate people to make it happen.

We'll explore in more depth in Part Two what defines a vision as 'compelling' and how to go about creating one. But it's worth arming yourself with knowledge of some of the reasons visions don't ignite the change you want to make.

A vision that isn't compelling enough

All visionary plans need a huge amount of dedicated effort to make them happen. If your vision isn't inspiring and exciting enough to tap into your colleagues' emotions, it won't energize them sufficiently. They need to feel it's worth their while to put their time and resources into this new project.

A compelling vision also needs to sell itself. When your seniors see it they must be convinced it's both achievable and transformational. By painting a vivid picture of what you want your customer experience to look like and giving them a couple of key points they can discuss with their peers on the board, you can make your vision work hard for you by drawing attention and resources towards it. When we say 'paint a picture', we mean that almost literally, in that by its nature a vision is a visual creature. We've seen many customer experience vision statements that are little more than spreadsheets with some generic statements such as 'we want to solve our customers' problems', or PowerPoint presentations seen by only 20 people that then go no further. If the pitching of a vision is non-visual and uninspiring, nothing will change.

Articulating the vision is only part of the job

Coming up with a vision that everyone can buy into feels like such a mammoth task that it can be tempting, once you've done it, to sit back and relax, assuming some major achievement has taken place. When this happens it's usually because the vision has been created by a core team who've thought of it as an isolated project rather than as the first step in a longer-term process. Have we got a vision? Tick – that's my objective done for the year. But unless there's a process that picks up the vision and runs with it, it will fizzle out. Creating the vision is the spark that ignites change, but it has a limited life of its own.

A vision is like yoghurt: it has a shelf-life. If you take too long trying to come up with your grand vision and are too slow in shifting it into a plan, it expires. We've worked with many clients who have been through several cycles of their vision, and because the right conditions weren't set, or they've not been able to move quickly enough to make it happen, it's lost its appeal and faded away. It no longer has relevance or commands attention.

As the number of people who need to understand and feel motivated by the vision grows, telling and re-telling the story becomes a near full-time job. Many businesses don't anticipate that effort, so they don't plan for it. The constant round of pitching and re-pitching of that vision exhausts them, and progress falters.

It's worth bearing in mind that translating a vision into reality also entails deciding what to *stop* doing, as well as what to do more of (or do for the first time). Because familiar activities feel safe, we humans are notoriously bad at giving them up. We argue the case for what we find easiest to do, rather than what's most likely to get us what we really want. In Part Two we'll talk more about the importance of translating the vision into a detailed plan, giving everybody a clear steer on the practical actions they need to take in their role while continually re-telling the story of why.

Setting the vision too far out

Where a vision sits in time is important. It should take you far enough into the future to feel worthwhile pursuing, but not so far ahead that it is dismissed as too ambitious, or is vulnerable to becoming irrelevant by the time it becomes reality. If your vision sits outside this timeframe it runs the risk of being lost among short-term fixes or sidelined as simply not a priority.

Many companies we've worked with have become highly sensitive to the need to be innovative and to their lack of pace, especially in their approach to technology. As a result, they want to push their thinking by setting their vision point 10 years into the future. However, although this longer-term scenario planning is essential for some businesses, 10 years is too far away for many in the organization to feel they can or want to affect it. And it's too hard to predict what will be needed 10 years from now. We recommend a vision that's three years out, with a 3- to 36-month rolling plan. It's worth developing an additional five-year picture, which helps senior people start thinking about the impact of new technologies and emerging consumer trends as these become more mainstream.

We have occasionally been challenged by our clients to be more ambitious with our vision for their business. And it's true that sometimes we've missed or underestimated the significance for their future service and experience of a trend or technology. However, pitching the vision with the right level of ambition is also about assessing what the organization and not just one ambitious individual feels able to take on. We're looking for what we call a 'pragmatic aspiration', which hits the right note with as many senior people as possible.

Difficulty imagining what the finished service will look like

Another challenge is that in some businesses no one team has a complete picture of what the customer experience is today and hence it's hard to imagine what it should be like. They may ask themselves: a vision for what? If you were to plan an extension for your house you'd have a vision of how you want it to appear when it's complete. That's because you know what your house looks like today, so you can imagine how it will be transformed by the changes. But with a service you might find it almost impossible to imagine exactly what you're trying to create a vision for, because you can't *see* the thing in its completeness today. This makes it hard to communicate internally, and therefore to make it into a reality.

For instance, if you're a retailer, when does your customer experience start and end? Is it from the moment your customers walk in the door to the time they leave the store, or does it start earlier than that – when they're thumbing through Pinterest, for instance? How about if they want to return something a month later – does it end then? If you're a bank, what's your vision for retail banking five years from now? It's not comprised only of what your website will look like or how you're planning to run your contact centres; it's those elements and more.

We worked with an insurance provider over eight or ten months to help them create a new vision. Before we arrived, the individual directors were becoming exasperated with themselves because although they knew what their objectives were, they were each imagining the solution as something different. For one, achieving the objective meant building webpages in a different way. For another, the solution was to develop a new digital product that would encourage customers to interact more with the brand. To another, a new business model and channel to market was needed. They had a massive opportunity to compete in their industry but couldn't organize themselves quickly enough, and as a result their momentum fragmented and they reverted to ad hoc adjustments to how they already operated. They spent their money putting paper forms online. This is what happens when it's hard to understand what the vision means to each area of the business and the business as a whole.

Who manages the whole process?

There probably isn't any one person or team in your organization who's responsible for managing the development of a holistic vision and strategy for the experience your customers have of your business. (You may have a Customer Strategy but this is likely to be focused on sales and not the experience.) Accountability for the customer may sit at the top of a vertical but responsibility for improving the experience for customers is distributed across several roles horizontally. If that cross-function responsibility sits at the top with the C-suite and it's organized, for example, into a Customer Board, then you're onto something. If that cross-functional group isn't coordinated or isn't senior enough or both, then it remains hard to form a coherent vision for the customer experience and harder to make it happen.

In the very worst of cases teams are, although well intentioned, battling each other for ownership of customer experience improvement. This well-mannered infighting happens when there is no shared understanding that the customer experience is in fact a shared responsibility requiring distinct endeavours, but in a coordinated way. In an early round of interviews with the stakeholders of one financial services company, it became clear that several people saw it as their responsibility to improve the experience for customers (which is great); however, they were also subtly critical or suspicious of the work of others. Before we could work to improve the design of their services we had to visualize for them the 'anatomy' of their currently disjointed customer experience programme and then how each part of what they were doing as individual teams could be organized as a coherent customer experience capability without the conflict.

We've met many dedicated people who attempt to get others excited by the notion of establishing a vision for their service, by running workshops and putting their case to those in charge, but when there wasn't anyone senior within the company asking for a vision, it wasn't going to go anywhere. These people needed to be able to convince those above them to give it priority, and they often lacked the tools to do so. (If this is you, this book will give you those tools.)

Unfortunately, many organizations still see the customer experience as the final element of delivering a service to a customer, rather than as something every element of the business is responsible for. Customer Experience Teams are often perceived as providing the 'cherry on the cake'. For this reason we encourage businesses to move their customer experience teams further up the hierarchy and give them resources and permission to establish projects across business areas.

It was exciting for us when the marketing director of one of our retail clients took their customer experience conversation to the board, making a case for the organization to work in a more customer-centric way. She succeeded, but it took us a year of practical project work and demonstrating the positive impact for customers to reach a point where enough of the middle management tier understood what was needed, and were confident enough to persuade their bosses. In the meantime, various teams around the business had been enthusiastically squirreling mini-projects back to their own departments – which of course was encouraging, but not nearly as effective as if all parts of the business had got behind the same vision in a coordinated effort.

Many factors can get in the way of making a vision into concrete change, so guiding your project sensitively and strongly from the beginning makes a significant difference. Without the right people giving it the right priority, and in the right way, you could end up with a sprinkling of diluted achievements rather than the bold transformation you were originally seeking and that your customers will notice and value. It often comes down to who has the sensitivity, the insight, and the curiosity to think about the customer and who has the authority and the mandate to effect change. It's not always the same person.

Key takeaways

- A service vision is a picture of a desired future state for your service, and for the experience you want your customers to have. You need one in order to make clear decisions about how to use your resources to delight your customers. A vision also helps everyone to pull in the same direction, avoiding the disjointed effect we talked about in the previous chapter. If you don't have one, you're likely to make a series of ad hoc improvements rather than a transformational change, with the risk that these make little positive impact on your customers.

- Most businesses find it hard to translate their vision into reality, thereby igniting meaningful change. There are six stumbling blocks inherent in this process:

  - There's confusion about what a vision is. What one person may see as a vision, another may think of as a set of corporate objectives, a strategy, a mission statement, or an action plan. In fact, a vision is none of these things; instead, it's the driving force behind them. Plans and objectives fall out of the vision, and are not a substitute for it.

  - You've created a vision that isn't compelling. Yours should be both complete and well-informed enough for your business to make decisions with it, and also exciting and realistic enough to convince them to make it happen.

  - Deciding on what the vision is, is only the first step. If it doesn't galvanize action quickly it will become more and more difficult to sell internally, leading to a tailing-off of action. Many businesses fail to sustain the momentum after the vision has first been articulated and shared.

- In an attempt to appear bold and ambitious, you may have set a vision with an end date too far into the future. Ten years is too long-term for most of your colleagues to get excited about, so stick to three or, at the most, five years.

- Given that services are hard to visualize even when they already exist, think how difficult it is to imagine what your service transformation will look and feel like for your customers several years into the future. Then multiply that by all the people in your organization who have a different take on it, and you can see how confusion can reign.

- Going back to our previous chapter where we talked about silos, it's unlikely that a single team will have responsibility for actioning the vision. This can result in disjointed implementation of it, especially if one senior authority isn't in control of the process.

The challenge of fast and slow   03

In his book *Thinking, Fast and Slow* (2012), the eminent psychologist Daniel Kahneman identifies two systems of judgement operating in our brains: System 1 and System 2. According to Kahneman, 'One system is fast, intuitive and emotional; the other is slower, more deliberative and more logical'. These systems seem to exist in organizations too. Neither system is wrong or right – in evolutionary terms we need both – but sometimes fast thinking, although attractive, can cause opportunities to be missed. Kahneman refers to the 'snap judgements' we make, which are based on beliefs we've established through our past experiences. These decisions can often be wrong, but we execute them because time is short and it's quicker to use the evidence we have to hand than to consider the longer-term, bigger picture. The world demands businesses move fast and be reactive, and yet this need for speed can also hinder their ambition and judgement (and, in practical terms, waste money).

Every organization experiences tension between the desire to move ahead at speed so as to achieve results quickly, and the need to play the long game in order to create a coordinated and lasting transformation. The challenge for organizations, as with human brains, is to find a way to allow the fast and slow to work together. Where this has a specific impact on transforming the customer experience is when it relates to the large number of people involved in delivering it and the challenge of changing a mindset and ways of working.

Every retail bank now has a banking app, which is improved continuously by new, in-house digital teams. The design and development of banking apps is now commonplace, yet the change behind the scenes has been much more significant. Some of these businesses have had to rebuild their banking platforms, they've had to rethink identification, authentication and data security, and they've had to reinvent a role for their branches and those that work in them. The vision for mobile digital banking was set more than 10 years ago following the invention of the smartphone and the senior executives who were asked to commit to this significant investment and change did so several years ago. As the apps have improved at pace through agile development, the organizations have been changing too, fundamentally, but at a slower pace. The pace they are able to achieve today was a long time in the planning.

In this chapter we'll identify some of the challenges of managing fast and slow together when it comes to getting new products and services to market. We'll describe how problems arise because all organizations contain many business functions and are staffed by people of different professional disciplines who have been hired to operate in different ways and have different priorities. We'll suggest that although 'agile management' is effective and is the right response to the speed of change we're all experiencing, some organizations have found that at scale, agile 'heads down' working can result in a lack of coordination and a focus on speed for speed's sake.

We'll argue that, of course, the answer lies in finding a balance; in setting the vision out there (but not too far) and then planning backwards to identify products to manage. We'll argue (and develop this argument in Chapter 7) that 'visioning' needs to be agile too.

We'll also hear from two of our clients at Dubai Airport. The team there has learned how to use design thinking and tools to manage an extreme case of 'fast and slow' – managing airport operations in the moment for thousands of passengers and dozens of flights each day, while at the same time planning the airport of the future.

What goes wrong when 'fast' and 'slow' progress aren't managed together?

When teams across a business have different views on how quickly their customer experience vision should be implemented, it becomes hard to determine what the new propositions and customer experience will be, and when they will be delivered. Digital people, for instance, will be asked to deliver tactical, incremental, and often uncoordinated improvements, which are nice to have but not always significant in terms of their impact in the market. At the same time, any attempts to implement more complicated, long-term, transformational change involving more investment and people never get off the ground, because everyone is focused on maintenance and quick fixes.

To help you see the contrast, picture this scenario. A company wants to create a seamless customer experience across its digital and in-store platforms. A meeting is held to kick off the project, attended by representatives from marketing, sales, technology, training and development, and operations. Marketing is raring to go, with ideas for a new website, digital marketing content and branding. Sales is also keen to make immediate changes, seeing this as an opportunity to increase short-term revenue. Training and operations, however, are more circumspect. They're considering the human implications of the transformation: the staff culture, engaging the retail operation, and the interface between the digital and 'bricks and mortar' parts of the customer operation. The technology team are excited by the opportunity to refresh the digital experience, but are also anxious about the state of the IT stack and the integration of systems required. This scenario isn't necessarily reflective of every business, but it illustrates how different organizational areas work at different speeds.

This fast and slow disconnect comes down to three main causes:

1 The cultural tension between those whose job roles require a view on the longer term, especially in parts of the operation that are harder to change, and those whose job roles don't require this.

2 The need to get quick results, particularly when senior people are focused and bonused on meeting sales targets.

3 The desire to change things too quickly while not taking account of the human scale of the change.

Culture clashes can impede progress

I'm sure you're familiar with the concept of *agile* product management, in which the aim is to get a new product or service produced as quickly as possible, refining it using early and continuous customer feedback. This is a movement that's sprung from software development, and in this world it makes total sense. It's possible to build software rapidly, test it, and then change it as quickly again; the world moves so fast that to spend months finessing an IT project creates a risk that the product will be obsolete before it's finished.

The problem arises when agile thinking is imported into traditional service-based organizations, creating a disconnect between those who naturally work in that way (usually the software developers brought in from outside to effect the digital changes) and those who don't. Understandably, designers and developers can get frustrated at the slow pace of those tasked with steering the super tanker of a people-based company through the uncharted waters of transformational change. All they want to do is make something, and as quickly as possible. However, what others want to do is work out how to get 100,000 employees to alter the way they manage and deliver the customer experience. It's like two gears at different speeds grinding against each other.

At the insurance company we mentioned in the last chapter, senior management had been trained in agile techniques whether they were software developers or not. As a result, liberated by not having to think things through too far ahead or jump through heavily gated project management process, they forged quickly ahead with the changes they wanted to make. But this way of working didn't match their organization's culture; a traditional insurance company will always have an extremely conservative attitude to risk and feel uncomfortable with delivering services that aren't signed off in triplicate. They had a layer of knowledge about agile, but lacked the culture to make it work. This tension between fast and slow led to uneven progress and internal disagreements, which in turn had a disabling effect on their customer experience programme.

Speed can become an end in its own right

For product development and management, agile management methods can work incredibly effectively. Once you've identified what you want your product to do, you can start to build it, test it, refine it, and eventually operate something you're happy with.

For a customer experience programme, however, agile working needs to be integrated into a strategic plan – with a clear vision. Our insurance company was so fixated on moving quickly it didn't do enough to define its vision at the beginning, which meant it didn't truly understand what business or customer proposition it wanted to create. Instead, it set itself up in agile teams under the illusion that fast and nimble was best. This blanket approach to the speed at which it felt it should work, together with the culture clash we mentioned above, led to outputs that weren't what you'd expect from an agile organization – traditional webpages with little personalization, for instance. People had thrown themselves into doing things quickly, without realizing that in some areas a slower, considered and vision-led approach is what's needed.

Although some at the start had seen the opportunity of a transformation step that would have resulted in not just a new website but a new direct-to-consumer line of business, the reality was a more contemporary-looking version of their current marketing website. They exhausted a lot of resources with no clear direction and lost time as a result.

Even if your industry is faster-moving than the insurance sector, you can see that, although agile working makes a lot of sense, simply speeding up isn't always going to work. For a start, it doesn't take account of how long *people* need to change their thinking and behaviour and what they need to believe to make change happen.

The present always feels more important until the future catches you out

Transport for London is an infrastructure business rightly focused on safety and reliability, and much of that infrastructure is decades old. Modernization is happening, but it takes time and is very costly. As Samantha describes:

The focus is ensuring we design experiences right the first time, that we deliver future-proofed products and services and avoid costly re-work or upgrades. Future-proofing means we have to anticipate what our customers will need and expect and we have to be able to make the case for longer-term solutions while we're fixing what we have. Defining and designing a clear end-state, even two years ahead, that our senior executives can sign up to is a vital step.

So for an organization like Transport for London, daily operations, safety and reliability are the focus. However, without a rolling two-year vision for customer service, they would not be able to anticipate future requirements or deploy innovation quickly enough, resulting in today's investments not being fit for purpose.

How can fast and slow be managed together?

Frank describes an extreme case of 'fast and slow' for Dubai Airports and how design thinking and tools were used to address three different levels of the problem:

The importance and complexity of striking a balance between fast and slow is particularly acute for major infrastructure providers such as Dubai Airports. In contrast to many other businesses, we forecast and plan long lead-time future facility requirements decades ahead, whilst in parallel needing to ensure our service levels remain responsive to customer needs and expectations on an hour-by-hour, day-by-day basis. The contrast between planning and developing far-future infrastructure requirements whilst remaining agile to near-term operational requirements is stark.

Dubai International is the busiest airport in the world in terms of international passenger numbers, with over 88 million passengers served in 2017.

As forecast demand growth exceeds the airport's ultimate potential capacity, the long-term plan is to continue to enhance Dubai International and in parallel develop Dubai Airports' secondary airport, Dubai World Central, into the hub airport of the future. On completion of all phases of development it is designed to be capable of serving up to 240 million passengers.

As part of developing the vision for the future of both airports, we had to start looking at our business differently, recognizing that to achieve the goals of both the future and the present we would have to change the way that planning and operations worked, with an emphasis on re-engineering how projects and initiatives were conceived, developed and implemented. We put in place a programme aimed at evolving beyond a provider of infrastructure into an innovative service company with hospitality and customer experience at its heart.

We knew that making customer experience the primary factor in everyone's decision-making, regardless of their role, would require time and patience. Our teams had been used to delivering and working in a certain way and we were now asking them to do things differently.

Given our multifaceted challenge we used the service design activity to tackle three things in parallel. The first was defining longer-term service concepts and the experience we wanted our airports to offer, and then defining the architecture (people, processes, systems, products) required to deliver this target experience.

The second was working out how we could work backwards from our future concept of experience to today's airport and understand what aspects were viable to be delivered into today's operation, to support us with today's challenges. The idea being that the activity and improvements of today would become stepping stones to enable us to start to build our aspirational capability of tomorrow.

The third thing was to understand what we needed to embed within our organization in order to achieve both these ambitions cohesively and in the quickest time possible.

What the team at Dubai Airports have demonstrated is the value of agile product development within the strategic framework of what we call an Experience Roadmap and developing the practice of Experience Portfolio Management. We'll describe these next.

Agile development within the framework of a vision

Large organizations are often great at project and programme delivery, organizing resources and managing interdependencies. But often the effect of that delivery, although optimal for the organization, doesn't feel very coordinated or excited from the outside. Much of the impact of programme delivery is on infrastructure and platforms and on incremental fixes and improvements to products.

Delivery programmes like this are essential. However, if you've spent the time defining a vision for your service and you've described and even visualized it, you may find that when you start speaking with delivery people about making it happen, your plan and theirs don't align.

We'll look in more depth in Part Two at ways to ensure your vision and service designs are ready to build and that the conditions are right. But here are two tangible ideas that illustrate how fast and slow can be managed together in the context of vision-led and customer-driven transformation.

Experience Portfolio

The idea of managing a portfolio is familiar in the world of change management, where projects and programmes are orchestrated to deliver change. Often, though, the idea of portfolio management is not applied in any holistic way to customer experience management and because it's not, the elements you've developed that together equal your vision for the service can get diluted, compromised or lost altogether. So the idea of an Experience Portfolio is to retain a sense that these elements work together – the sum is greater than the parts – and there are specific aspects of these solutions that will make it a success and that therefore should not be compromised.

Experience Roadmap

When an organization has many teams all working on aspects of the total experience for customers, it's very helpful to create and manage a single view of what the next 3 to 36 months will look and feel like for customers and agree this as the single reference point. An Experience Roadmap is different from a delivery programme, although they should inform each other. The aim of the Experience Roadmap is to ensure that the customer propositions and experiences that build towards the vision land in the market in a way that has impact – that changes how consumers perceive your brand and how customers buy. In one sense an Experience Roadmap is more like a marketing campaign plan than a delivery programme. It identifies when the customer will see and feel new propositions and experiences (when these will first launch and how they will scale). It's developed through a 'negotiation' between the vision for the service and the developing capabilities of the business. Once this Roadmap is scoped (and it will need continual adjusting), a delivery programme can be created beneath it.

Early results are vital in signalling that the intention to change is real

Adam has worked for both E.ON and the UK National Grid and in both organizations has sought to create customer-driven transformation. We first met when he was working with E.ON UK, a company that has had a Service Design team for around 10 years now. Adam talks about the failures as well as the successes:

> One of our early projects was to redesign the steps and the experience for new customers as they chose and signed up to E.ON as their energy supplier. The sales and on-boarding experience that we designed was well received by the business but most of the solutions required big changes to IT systems.

The problem, as Adam put it, was 'We didn't do enough to pull out the quick wins'. Following a flurry of creativity, energy and goodwill, teams and organizations can lose interest very quickly and revert to ad hoc fixes.

The client team at E.ON decided they needed to go back a step and identify the things that people could just get on with while the case for systems change could be made and the work done. It's important that what are often called 'quick wins' are clearly identified and understood as being as valuable as the solutions that will make significant differences for customers in the mid- and longer-term.

'You need to do things quickly to build and sustain the momentum.' Adam cited the need to establish behaviours to drive the change. Once the vision is set and new services and experiences have been defined, people need to get going; things need to feel real quickly. And getting early results that are steps towards the vision will help you to make the case for further investment and validate the approach you're taking.

Key takeaways

- Agile ways of working are now standard in many organizations, or at least in certain parts of them. This has created an influx of new, increasingly customer-responsive services.

- Attempting to combine long- and short-term plans creates a particular challenge for service design. Everyone likes quick results, but some aspects of delivering a service simply can't be rushed.

- This can cause internal conflict, especially when different business teams have their own views about how fast their customer experience vision should be implemented. The difficulties centre around these factors:

  - culture clashes between people working in different disciplines, which can impede progress;

  - the pressure to achieve results quickly in order to meet sales or savings targets, which can lead to speed becoming an end in its own right;

  - a lack of attention being paid to the complex human elements of change, especially when large numbers of customer service staff are involved.

- Managing fast and slow together is the answer. This can be done by carrying out agile product and service development within a strategic framework that ensures the original vision is kept intact. Experience Portfolios bring together all aspects of the new customer experience, both short and long term. And Experience Roadmaps create a single timeline for what implementation will look like from the customer's perspective (this is distinct from conventional approaches to programme planning, which tend to sequence implementation based on available internal resources and commercial priorities alone).

- Creating some quick wins early on in your project signals that the organization is committed and keeps people motivated.

Reference

Kahneman, D (2012) *Thinking, Fast and Slow*, Penguin, London

The challenge of emotion   04

In the last 10 years, technological advances have enabled businesses to become increasingly efficient in their operations. Instead of an online travel operator answering our query in its expensive call centre, it's got us talking to a chat bot; instead of talking to a car salesman we're choosing interior fabrics and accessories and buying cars online. We're requesting more of our prescription drugs without visiting our doctor; we can travel through an airport with only our passport and our smartphone (and soon only our smartphones and our faces).

If your company has followed suit this is great news for your bottom line, as it's allowing you to cater for your customers at lower cost. This stream-lining of service delivery is also welcomed by your customers, as it removes unnecessary processes for them. There are times, though, when it's easy to feel the pendulum has swung too far. That's not to say we'd want to go back to the days when everything was done in person and by hand, but once all the human interaction is designed out we're left with little or no emotional connection to the businesses and services we use.

What's more, now that most companies transact with customers much more efficiently, it's ceasing to be the competitive advantage it once was. Once the transactions are frictionless or even invisible to your custom-ers, what is it that stops them leaving for one of your equally frictionless competitors? Whether customers ask for it or not, is there in fact a commer-cial imperative to design-in some moments of human connection with your brand? After decades of designing the humanity out of their systems, busi-nesses are starting to ask the vital question: where did the emotion go?

According to the authors of an article entitled, 'The new science of customer emotions', 'When companies connect with customers' emotions, the payoff can be huge' (Magids, Zorfas and Leemon, 2015). As evidence they cite several examples, including a major bank that launched a credit card product targeted at Millennials that was specifically designed to connect emotionally with the demographic. The bank saw an uplift in use of the credit card of 70 per cent and an overall growth in the value of transactions of 40 per cent. The article shows that a customer who is emotionally engaged with your brand is more valuable to you than one who is only satisfied. The authors propose that understanding 'emotional motivators' should be considered 'a science – and a strategy' for organizations. The emphasis of the article is on using data and analytics to profile your customers in order to target marketing messages. For us what's even more interesting is how to design responses to customers' emotional motivators into the fabric of a service proposition and to realize them in the experience customers have.

In this chapter we make the case for understanding human emotions as inspiration for good service design and the development of valuable propositions. We suggest the qualities of a service and experience that can trigger positive emotions for those using them – and that these triggers can be designed-in. We explain why businesses find it hard to work with emotions, how they get better at it and how they benefit when they do.

Why do we forget the emotion?

Services are woven into the human condition, so let's tap into that emotion. Have you thought about why people really use your service… *really* why they use it? No, really? When you work on the inside and you're delivering against your objectives it's easy to forget to ask this fundamental question. We humans are emotional creatures; pretty much everything we choose is in response to our feelings. Even the most rational-seeming of purchase decisions, such as our choice of electricity supplier, has an emotional component: it feels good to get a great deal, doesn't it? This has profound implications for how service industries design the triggers of positive emotion into the delivery of their customers' experiences. In the hotel industry, for instance, Forrester's Customer Experience Index shows 90 per cent of customers who feel valued will advocate for that brand; in the TV service provider industry, which has the largest percentage of customers who feel annoyed compared to any other industry, only 8 per cent will do so. Emotions matter to business performance (Milligan, 2016).

We know as customers ourselves that we prefer to deal with organizations that appear to understand us, share our values, and endear themselves to us in some way. We give our loyalty to those who succeed in this. And yet, although we understand the importance of emotional connection, when we get to work most of our efforts are focused on improving the rational, transactional parts of the service and experience. It's as if we travel to work as living, breathing and emotional beings, only to turn into logical robots as soon as we step into the office.

Why is it such a challenge for us to maintain that essential focus on emotion when we design our customer experience journey? There are three main reasons:

- Emotion is hard to quantify, measure and predict.
- Embedding emotion into the customer experience takes time.
- Many businesses have a cultural paradigm that has never included taking emotion seriously as a commercial driver.

The triggers of positive emotions can be designed-in

As service designers, we look to create an emotional response in the people experiencing a service by designing-in whatever is needed to engender that response. It could be how the service looks, feels and sounds when a customer is experiencing it, often through moments that delight and surprise them. To create positive feelings, we need to know which ones we want to encourage so we can design them in from the beginning. If we can achieve this, customers will feel more of an affinity towards the service.

Consciously designing the moments and the mechanisms to provoke a positive emotional response when someone uses your service is critical. But what are the qualities of a great service that tend to give your customers a positive experience? Consider these:

- **Reliable:** performing well again and again, and being trustworthy.
- **Helpful:** making tasks easy to complete, and resolving your customers' problems quickly.
- **Relational:** knowing and remembering your customers and their preferences, and being interested in a long-term relationship.
- **Distinct:** being original, authentic and clear about the expression of your brand.
- **Timely:** never being intrusive but always on hand.
- **Nurturing:** developing the skills and confidence of your customers, while delivering the service they've paid for.
- **Collaborative:** designing dialogue into the service and allowing your customers to participate, even designing new products and services with you.

- **Harmonious:** helping your consumers to experience a well-orchestrated performance, with all touchpoints and channels working together in a such a way that they feel in control.
- **Thoughtful:** anticipating, understanding and satisfying your customers' needs and desires.
- **Elegant:** lacking complication and needing little explanation – less is more.
- **Beautiful:** looking and feeling attractive.

Some of these qualities simply involve making sure the service does what it says it's going to do – it's pretty basic stuff. However, in many industries this is still a differentiator. For instance, many organizations promise a simple online sign-up procedure, which then turns out to be anything but, annoying their users not only because their time is being wasted, but also because they were given a promise that wasn't kept.

We could do more to quantify feelings

Most businesses are numbers-driven – they must be. And feelings, by their very nature, aren't easily packaged up into numerical bundles. As a result, companies rarely track or measure their customers' emotional reactions along with the plethora of other customer satisfaction factors in their regular research efforts. This can make it tricky to build a business case to prove the worth of a more emotionally attuned customer experience – a situation that is exacerbated by the fact that many businesses who do want to learn how their customers feel are often measuring the wrong things.

What's more, emotional measurement requires a more open approach to research. A company might have plenty of customer satisfaction data that tells it what's liked and disliked about its website, but this doesn't necessarily reveal what underlies those feelings. Its customer experience team will therefore find it hard to interpret the figures, graphs and charts because it doesn't know why its customers feel the way they do, or where it should set the satisfaction baseline. To what and to whom are their customers comparing the company? If it were to ask broader questions such as, 'What do people expect from us?' or, 'What do they believe about the kind of services we offer?' it might learn more. In other words, if all it knows is that its customers are not keen on its online presence, it's not discovering what it really needs to know; instead, it's stuck in the purgatory of a short and poorly informed feedback loop.

A 2016 survey (Temkin Group, 2016) of 10,000 US consumers provided evidence for a correlation between the 'delight' felt by customers following their experience of a business and their likelihood to: buy more (87 per cent of delighted customers), trust and recommend the company (87 per cent), try new things (65 per cent) and forgive the business when they made a mistake (71 per cent). Notably, when customers felt 'upset' by their experience these percentages each dropped to around 10 per cent.

An understanding of your customers' emotions can be translated into practical tools and made more predictable

Like anything else, innovating with the emotional element of the customer experience involves trialling a series of initiatives so you can measure and understand the response. Just as a retailer can predict the increased sales they'd get by discounting a certain item, you would want to do the same when you invest in building emotion into your customer journey.

The problem is, it's almost impossible to predict the 'return on investment' of an emotional response. Just as music producers have tried for years without success to identify the formula for a number one hit, when you create some theatre in your service or make it a treat to use, you never know exactly how your customers are going to react until you try it. What's more, it might not increase sales directly, but could still improve customer retention and share of transactions. That's a quantifiable result, but not as easy to hang your hat on as a direct sales increase.

So what can be done about this? As part of our work with a super grocer in the UK, we developed a 'Needs Dashboard'. For this, we researched and identified 30 distinct tasks or activities that their customers did as they interacted with the brand. To be clear, this wasn't limited to buying food. Customers also plan, they look for inspiration, they try or trial the supermarket's products and services, and so on. Once we'd established this long but universal set of customer tasks, we wrote an 'experience requirement' against each. In other words, we described what we felt customers wanted the experience of completing that task (and fulfilling a need) to be.

The needs fell into three categories:

1 Those needs that we knew would be important to customers because they were the things they consciously expected a supermarket to do well, for example, having the products in stock and making it easy to pay.

2 Those needs that customers felt added to the experience, for example, stores, websites and product ranges that were easy to navigate and finding it easy to get help in-store and online.

3 Lastly, and because this framework was there to drive behaviours within the business, we included a set of needs that we anticipated would become more valuable as mainstream consumer behaviour caught up with emerging expectations. We also knew that for the business to achieve its brand repositioning it would need to make fulfilling these needs a strategic point of difference.

We completed some qualitative research to understand whether our client's customers did in fact have these needs. The research helped us to identify the needs of its customers that the company should prioritize when designing and delivering its services. We were then able to identify gaps in what the company was currently measuring, showing that although they gathered a lot of data, the data couldn't tell them whether or not they were doing the things their customers needed and valued most. With the priority needs and the relevant sources of data in place, we developed a Customer Needs Dashboard, eventually owned by the Marketing Director, and reported each week alongside the commercial Marketing and Sales dashboard.

Working with Sean at Bupa we created several tools that helped senior stakeholders and delivery teams understand the shift in emotional responses that we wanted customers to have as a result of redesigning their patient journey. As Sean describes it:

> Our design guiderails included our service vision, a set of five promises we want to keep every time for every customer, and 13 design principles. But it also included for each step of each journey a description of the shift in how we wanted customers to feel. These before and after statements are so important. So, for example, when customers confirm cover we wanted the experience to shift from 'moments of doubt about the extent to which I am covered' to 'an effortless and reassuring clarification that reminds you of what you're covered for so there are no surprises'.

Emotional embedding takes time

Certain industries have spent years educating their consumers to focus purely on price. Credit cards are a brilliant example of this; they draw in account holders with a 0 per cent interest rate for six months, at which point the cardholder jumps ship to another discounted card. Like the credit card companies, many businesses have embedded the need to offer the best value for money into their company culture, which makes it hard for them to explore emotional value, engendering an emotional connection with customers, as a commercial advantage.

And yet, the realization that positive feelings are something people will pay extra for is now starting to become prevalent. Take the supermarket sector, which has believed for the past 10 years that price is the most important thing for its customers. The problem for most grocery chains is they'll never be the cheapest, so now they're focusing more on the human value side of the equation as a point of difference. The challenge for them lies in redesigning their services to create a positive emotional response, at the same time as 'retraining' their customers to value those soft benefits. It's a tall order.

So you can only move as fast as your customers want to change their minds. This presents a hurdle for businesses, because altering consumers' ingrained assumptions is slow and laborious and requires a huge amount of patience and consistency.

And furthermore, you have to re-educate your colleagues too. Sean from Bupa brings this point to life:

> I love my job. Who wouldn't? I turn up each day wanting to do great things for our customers and our people. But you need to engage with colleagues both rationally and emotionally. Everyone in the organization needs to understand that what is good for the customer is good for the business. But often it's the emotional connection – really putting yourself in the customer's shoes – that commits people to change. Very rarely can you change the behaviour of staff using Excel or PowerPoint.

There is no Head of Emotions or Chief Emotions Officer

Making a profit is every company's priority – even more so if it experiences a sudden drop in sales or its closest competitor posts better than expected results. Understandably, in those scenarios, it will be tempted to slap together a quick fix for the problem by implementing discounts or promotions, rather than by embedding more emotion in the customer experience. The financially led response is fast, easy and relatively safe, which makes it simple to make a case for. CEOs and directors feel like they're doing something constructive to solve the immediate business issue. Emotions, on the other hand, are less concrete and easy to justify, which means in most businesses, conversations based on what they want their customers to feel, rather than to spend, don't get the same attention.

Interestingly this isn't the case when it comes to their advertising budget. Most large businesses acknowledge the power of emotion when advertising their brand. Think of the car industry: cars are essentially pieces of engineering, produced with performance, safety and efficiency in mind. Yet their advertising is pure emotion, crafting a story to convince their customers the car is somehow going to change their lives. It's as if the car maker has outsourced the emotion to its ad agency.

In fact, it's worth looking at the contrast between the manufacturing and service sectors in terms of where emotion sits in the customer experience. A manufactured product is designed and created well before it's experienced by the customer, with the emotional qualities having been embedded in the design at some previous point in time. In our car example, vehicle designers will have made the seating and dashboard feel premium, and the exterior look like a sculpture on wheels, well before the customer has bought and experienced those emotional touches for themselves.

A service, on the other hand, connects emotionally with its customers at the point of production. The management of people's emotions in the moment is what the customer service industry is built on. A customer complaints team, for instance, will try to neutralize people's negative feelings; a hotel will want to help guests feel relaxed and important. It's a relatively new approach, however, to consciously design the mechanisms for a positive emotional response into a service right from the beginning; to programme it into the technologies that underlie delivery and to recruit and train it into the people on the frontline. In the automotive sector the service happens in the retail stores (or dealerships) and in the vehicle servicing workshop around the back.

Our client Yeonhee Lee from the Hyundai Motor Company describes how designing-in that emotional connection has real commercial benefits. She told us:

> The Hyundai Motor Company is determined to be the world's best for service in the automotive industry, which is not an industry always synonymous with great customer service. It's important to understand that we see 'service' not 'sales' as the basis of valuable customer relationships. If we give people a great experience they will buy from us.
>
> Engine helped us to imagine and design a ground-breaking retail experience for our new retail experience model, Hyundai Motorstudio in Gangnam. We looked at a site in Dosan neighbourhood in Seoul to design and build a brand experience space. We opened it and had 200,000 visitors in the first 18 months, which was over four times what we'd expected. Most significantly we've been able to create a cultural space, one that communicates the values of the Hyundai Motor Company brand and reflects the needs and expectations of a younger market. Our approach has been to understand what it means to people to buy a car and to connect with the values and aspirations of a younger and wealthier group of consumers.

The service model developed for Hyundai Motorstudio has been expanded into various regions worldwide. It's also been a leading practice in the automotive industry; thus many competitors have kept watching our performance and next steps.

Figure 4.1 Hyundai Motorstudio in Gangnam, Seoul was designed to be a cultural destination, attracting a younger than usual audience with events and exhibitions

Key takeaways

- Developments in the automation of customer service delivery have led to reduced costs and, in many cases, a smoother experience for all concerned. But this has come at a price, which is the reduction or removal of the emotional connection between your business and your customers.

- Rather than being a hindrance, human feelings can be an inspiration for service design.

- Brilliant services help us to lead more enjoyable and productive lives. Therefore, when you tune in to and trigger positive emotions with your services, the benefits are more fully appreciated by your customers.

- The problem is, businesses find it hard to 'deal' with emotion, and tend to focus on the rational and functional aspects of service design and performance. This is because emotions are hard to quantify and measure; they can be complicated to embed into a service and traditionally most companies have never been good at doing this.

- Emotion can be 'designed-in' to services in numerous ways, ensuring that a service either meets the customer's basic needs, or that it's a differentiator. When a service presses the emotional buttons by being thoughtful, elegant, helpful, delightful and even nurturing and supportive, it's likely to be trusted more and tolerated when things don't work as they should.

- Bringing emotion into your service can be achieved in several ways:
  - Doing more to quantify emotional responses to a service, for instance through consumer research.
  - Developing tools to understand and predict customers' emotions.
  - Accepting that embedding emotional triggers into services and ways of working takes time.
  - Imagining and designing-in the mechanisms for triggering positive emotional response to a service from the beginning; the same effect can't be achieved following launch with emotional marketing.

References

Magids, S, Zorfas, A and Leemon, D (2015) The new science of customer emotions, *Harvard Business Review*, November

Milligan, V (2016) A closer look at the monetary value of emotion, Forrester Blogs, 21 September. Available online at: http://blogs.forrester.com/victor_milligan/16-09-20-a_closer_look_at_the_monetary_value_of_emotion

Temkin Group (2016) 2016 Temkin Experience Ratings, Temkin Group, March

The challenge of distinctiveness 05

Imagine you're boarding a plane to your next holiday destination. Squeezing yourself down the aisle past the passengers and cabin crew, you manage to ram your hand baggage into the overhead locker and collapse into your seat. Finally, you allow yourself the luxury of congratulating yourself on booking a flight to the sun at such a bargain price – what on earth did you do before budget airlines came along? When you think about it, how amazing is it that you can fly halfway across the continent for the cost of a train fare at home? As you rearrange your elbows to avoid contact with the person next to you, you start to plan your first day abroad. What will it be, beach or pool?

At that moment something strange happens. A smiling member of the cabin crew approaches with a tray of champagne and offers a glass to you. What's this? Gingerly you accept the drink and – yes – it's the real thing. This is nice! Except… it feels slightly wrong. Why would a low-cost airline be dishing out expensive drinks when they're supposed to be a 'no frills' outfit? You don't want to complain, but if they've got money to burn then possibly your ticket isn't as good value as you'd thought. On the other hand, maybe they're buttering you up before they announce a four-hour wait on the tarmac. Why else would they be so generous?

Just like this airline, every company wants its service to be perceived differently from that of its competitors, and yours is no different. But just standing out isn't good enough – your service needs to be quintessentially *yours*. You want your customers to come away from experiencing your service not only feeling delighted that they went to you, but also remembering your brand as being an integral part of it. This airline created a disconnect between its brand expression and its service proposition that left you feeling ill at ease.

In this chapter we'll explore the challenge of making your service and the experience for your customers distinctive. We suggest that there is currently a power-play in many large organizations between the Brand Team and the Customer Experience Team for control of your customers' perception of your business. And we'll define 'service proposition' as being distinct from 'brand proposition'.

How brand expression has given way to customer experience

First, a little history. When we first started in service design around the time of the millennium, most companies worked on the assumption that what made them distinctive was their brand. It was also around this time that they started to realize that those brands weren't only comprised of their logo and colours, but much more. So mobile phone companies, for instance, started to move beyond their visual identities: in the UK, mobile operator Orange was talking about the future being 'bright', Telefonica (O2 in the UK) was about being a liberating breath of fresh air, and Vodafone carried a sense of assuredness and credibility for a corporate world. These points of difference came from investing in what was at the time called 'brand expression'.

Services are naturally differentiated, of course. If you were to walk down your local high street and check out the first five small hairdressers you came across, you'd find that although they offer similar services in similar environments, they manage to distinguish themselves from each other through the personalities of their owners and staff. No input from expensive branding consultancies has been required there. Like the hairdressers, the brand personalities of larger companies used to emerge unconsciously out of their business priorities, the culture set by their founders, and as a by-product of the products and services they sold. The last few decades saw the management of brands transform from an art to very much a science.

Fast-forward to today, and your *customer experience*, rather than your brand, is the shortcut to how your customers evaluate what they think and feel about your business. This means your brand can have the most stunning logo, the most impactful ad campaign, or the lowest prices, but none of that guarantees your customers will feel good about spending money with you. I'm sure you can think of many brands that promote themselves in an appealing way but don't provide a likeable service experience, and as we saw with the low-cost airline story, when there's a disconnect between what a business wants you to believe and what you actually experience, this creates a lack of trust in your mind.

Moving from 'brand expression' to 'your customer experience is your brand'

You can take a more fundamental approach to distinctiveness than by simply expressing your brand's personality through the physical design of the touchpoints with your service. This approach requires creating or revisiting your service proposition and the offers that deliver it, and recasting this service as the core of your brand. Expressing your brand personality through the design of your customer touchpoints is 'distinctiveness level one', while designing your service proposition in a way that engenders the right perceptions of your business in your customers' minds is 'distinctiveness level two':

Level one: translating your brand personality into service aesthetics and behaviours. A hospitality business that has 'fun' as a core brand value could translate that brand value into how their hotels are designed (bright colours), what their staff wear (casual and bright uniforms) and behave like (friendly and upbeat), and how their website works (great photography and lots of movement). This is what we meant earlier by 'brand expression'.

Level two: creating a service proposition that delivers your organization's strategic objectives in a way that's both desirable and useful for your customers.

Here's where it gets more sophisticated and interesting than level one. In defining your service proposition, you're actually defining your brand from the outside-in, because increasingly your customers' experience *is* your brand. To do this you'll identify what we (and others) call 'hallmarks', which are material points of distinction in what you offer and how you offer it that may have implications for your operating model. These could be elements such as distribution channel, pricing, offers, or features of your service that together deliver your central proposition. It's likely these will stem from your core competencies and capabilities, or those you can invest in.

So, our imagined hospitality business might focus, for example, on creating a sense of membership of likeminded people who see travel as life-enhancing, and site hotels only in the 'centre of the action', focusing on cities that are known for their nightlife. They could build elements of surprise (only nice ones) into the guest experience and reward loyalty with tickets to local 'fun' entertainment venues. The people they employ in their hotels would be a hallmark too. 'Fun' isn't 'stupid' or 'flippant' but the hotel staff will be comfortable talking to guests and putting them at ease. They'll be the kind of people who can recommend a local bar or venue (even if they don't live nearby) and use what they've learned about their guests to tailor their stay.

So level two is about designing points of distinction into the fabric of the service model, offerings, promises and benefits (the service proposition). These are aspects that are more fundamental (and therefore harder to copy) than appearances and generic customer service behaviours.

When we worked with the Hyundai Motor Company in Seoul, their brand positioning was clear, but they wanted our help in translating this into a retail experience model they could pilot in a new brand space. We used spaces and technology to create moments within the environment of the six-story site encapsulating the modern and premium values of the brand. For instance, we created an art exhibition space and library for the store. In this library, visitors have access to a series of rare and significant collections of books about cars; these books are difficult to find elsewhere in Korea, making it a 'go-to' place for any car enthusiasts. They have an excellent experience of configuring their car and, if they want to learn more, the new 'Gurus' have some great tools to help customers understand the build quality of Hyundai's vehicles. Moreover, the brand space offers cultural programmes such as 'Dialogue with Car' on a regular basis, where visitors are invited to meet and connect with the likes of the engineers, designers and car racers from Hyundai Motors.

We worked closely with the client team in Hyundai to redesign the role and approach of the retail staff. This was, in fact, the greatest challenge. The staffing model, management and approach to customer service was like that of many car dealerships: very traditional and very conservative. This system reflected an important tradition, not only for those who sold the cars but also for those who, until recently, had bought them. The staff and culture mirrored that of the traditional Hyundai customer. By designing with sales staff at the company, we were able to define (and negotiate) the new roles and behaviours that were needed to draw in a younger and increasingly wealthy audience – a vital outcome for the business.

This illustrates how, when we work with businesses to develop their service proposition, we pinpoint a small number of elements for them to invest in. These elements are chosen because they exemplify the values and personality of the brand most strongly. Together it's these elements that allow customers to have an experience that feels like an expression of the brand and is distinctive alongside the competition. Deciding on these elements involves far more than simply asking, 'Here are our brand values. How do we translate them into how our website operates, or how the insides of our stores look?' That's level one. Rather, it means taking a few steps back and asking, 'What's our offering? What's our proposition? Moreover, which parts of it will distinguish us from our competitors' propositions?' The result is that rather than being just another car showroom, this store is now a stop on the cultural tour of the area.

Today, consumers are paying less attention to what you say about yourself as a brand (in other words, your brand expression) and more to what you actually *are* and *do*. If your brand has innovation as a core value, for instance, are you solving your customers' day-to-day problems in a truly inventive and new way? And is this obvious to them? These are questions that, traditionally, brand and advertising agencies don't provide effective answers to, because their focus is on the outward projection of the brand – on 'telling' not 'acting'. They don't have the technical service know-how to help their clients 'hardwire' points of distinction into the operation of the service. On the other hand, the creation and delivery of a 'hallmark' requires detailed design to deliver it consistently and naturally.

We think the days of simply focusing on the communication of a brand message are gone – or certainly this has become much less important by comparison. Your customers buy utility, reliability and the ability to do what they want with your service. So when you talk about points of distinction, it's helpful to go back to something more fundamental than how your brand appears. Digging deeper will enable you to find those values that are tangible for your customers when they experience your service. To do this requires both lateral thinking and a solid understanding of what your customers get from you and what they really value. So, what defines your purpose in your customers' lives; what are the tangible proof points (not the ad campaigns) that will ensure they believe it too?

The service proposition

We work with some great brands, and they all spend a lot on marketing. The marketing focuses on what their brand *says*, but central to what a brand *does* is its service proposition. For example, when we worked with a European automotive brand we researched what customers considered when they got their car serviced with this manufacturer. We discovered that uncertainty about the bill made them anxious. So, we designed a set of fixed price packages, which went on to become a subscription model. When we helped a major consumer brand open a hotel for the first time in the US, we learned that business travellers, who spend much of their lives in hotels, would love the hotel they visited often to feel more like a home from home. So, we designed a way for guests' rooms to have the media and settings they wanted ready and waiting for them, with regular guests being offered the option to leave their personal items with the hotel ready for their next stay. And when we worked with an airport group serving the country's coastal tourism market, we found out that families with children were desperate for services that catered for them. So, we focused on airport services and environments that created an emotional connection between the airport and its travellers with small children. These became the proof points for its claim to 'family friendliness' by, for example, loaning children's strollers to parents for them to use after they'd checked in their own.

When we work with organizations we often discover that they don't have a single, simple and shared understanding of the service proposition they have today or are trying to create. We work through the early parts of the design process to a point where we can agree together how to describe and depict the target proposition on a single page. Most often we depict it as a Vision Wheel (see Chapter 10).

So how do you ensure your customers' experience of your service is noticeably different from your competitors? Ask yourself: what are the five or six things that make your service distinctly 'you'? Suppose your service contains a technological benefit over and above your competitors' offerings – that's an easy point of difference. However, to make it a differentiator, you'd need to get your frontline staff so excited about it that they can't help but communicate it as a tangible benefit to your customers. The ability to surprise and delight is also important; even within the design of a phone call or an interaction with someone in one of your retail stores, you can invest in creating a handful of touches you want your customers to recognize and remember as synonymous with your business and no other.

We've worked for many years with a major telecoms and media provider in the UK, including the development of a successful programme designed to ensure their customers get excellent service from any of the staff they encounter. Importantly, we've helped to ensure that beyond the great service it offers, the 10 per cent that makes the experience distinct is defined clearly and well implemented. To do this, we sat alongside the sales and customer care teams answering the phones, the people in the stores, and the engineers on the trucks that visit customers in their homes. With each channel, we went through a design process to create a framework of behaviours for great service and identified a small number of focus areas – the 10 per cent. For example, for customer care in the contact centre, we concentrated on teams and systems investment to enable four specific behaviours:

1 Show the customer we know them, and use what we know to anticipate what they might be calling about.

2 Make sure the customer doesn't have to call us again. We can do this by checking the common repeat drivers list, or telling them about 'self-care' options that might help them in future.

3 Surprise the customer by doing something that saves them money, or helps them get more from our products.

4 Make a specific reference to the customer's situation, story, or the products they've chosen, while signing off.

These behaviours might seem obvious or too subtle to count for much, but the narrow focus is important when a call centre agent only has a few minutes to be the voice of the brand on the phone. And the challenge of ensuring these people can do even these little things well every time is surprising. Each channel has its own pointers for distinctive interactions with customers, as each one is different and interacts with customers at different points in their end-to-end journey. For an engineer entering someone's home to behave in a way that's distinctly branded, for instance, requires a different approach from someone selling products in a store.

Of course, having a clear idea of your own distinctiveness and ensuring it's translated into what your people say and do achieves more than simply positioning yourself against your current competitors. It also makes it easier for you to distinguish yourself in a market liable to entry from new competition. Once you have control over what makes you different, you're able to deliver your services with confidence both now and in the future.

Why do we find it hard to create truly distinctive services?

Now you understand the difference between a service that is expressed only through its superficial projection (its logo, colours and so on) and that which is truly distinct through the experience its customers have of it, why are so many service providers not managing this effectively? There are four main challenges that businesses struggle with.

It can be easy to confuse your brand proposition with your service proposition and hard to align them

As we've already seen, many companies muddle the superficial expression of a brand with its lived experience in its customers' eyes. This is the difference between a brand proposition and a service proposition. The Virgin Group illustrates this challenge at the extreme. It's something founder Richard Branson has spoken about at length, and we've also had the advantage of seeing it from the inside while working with the marketing directors of three of the Virgin group of businesses. Branson's Virgin empire began in 1970 as a record store, with the company name chosen provocatively to signal a naive level of entrepreneurialism. He and his two co-founders were defiantly anti-establishment, and wanted to be what are today called industry disruptors. Their boldest move came early on, by deciding that in addition to selling music they would also operate an airline, Virgin Atlantic (one of our first clients). They shaped their entrepreneurialism into consumer championing, taking on the establishment in several other industries.

Today the Virgin Group comprises around 30 companies worldwide, spanning travel, hospitality, telecoms and media, health, and of course space travel. Virgin sees the truest expression of the spirit of the original music label in Virgin Atlantic, which combines anti-establishment business practices with fun and glamour. However, you can't think about Virgin (health) Care, Virgin's low-cost UK mobile network, or their bank, in the same way as you can their airline. Air travel is exciting and potentially glamorous, while medical testing and treatments, getting a statement from your bank, or paying your phone bill, are not. It's no easy matter for Virgin to translate the spirit of the Virgin brand proposition into well-honed service propositions in each of these diverse sectors.

The Virgin Group has a conscious awareness of these issues and as a result has very strong brand leadership and very experienced brand managers who continually monitor and advise the brand teams in each Virgin business. As a result, each Virgin business in whichever sector, from health to broadband internet, has a Virgin element in its brand DNA and a style of service delivery that sets it apart from the established brands in that sector. But you can see how in a business with less understanding of the difference between a service proposition and a brand proposition, confusion could ensue.

Linking your brand's points of distinction to your business strengths

The easiest way to annoy your customers is to give them high expectations that you can't match. Developing a positively distinctive service comes from marrying your brand ambitions with your organization's capability to deliver them. This potential dissonance between the shiny presentation of a branded service and the reality for your customers can even become headline news. Some huge corporations have been heavily criticized by governments, and satirized in the media, for saying one thing and being another. In the UK, utility providers nPower, E.ON Energy and Vodafone have been fined in recent years by their regulators for, respectively: failing to bill their customers on time (or at all); not setting customers up with the lowest tariff when they were required to do so; and not achieving the mobile network coverage they'd advertised. Each of these businesses had, in the same years, emphasized their customer focus in their marketing. It would have helped them better if they had focused their campaigns on aspects of their operation and offering that they could deliver brilliantly, and developed features that would delight their customers even without significant investment.

You might be in an organizational bubble

Companies often assume, for instance, that one of their main points of difference is the people in their customer contact centre. But do they know that to be true? They might believe it is because they once won a customer service award, but they probably haven't counted how many awards their competitors have won; the idea that they're the best at frontline service has therefore grown as an internal myth. The challenge is to find genuine points of distinction that everyone can agree on, which can be extremely difficult when it involves turning internal assumptions into outside-in reality checks. These points of distinction may be slight; they may be based in the peculiarities of your operating model or the heritage of your business. If one or some can be found, you may need to invest to amplify their effect for your colleagues and your customers.

It's natural to want to hang on to everything

You know the routine. After many hours of meetings your marketing team finally decides, 'Our main points of difference are that we're totally transparent and want to be the customer champion in our industry. We will also make our pricing fair.' This sounds like a great set of distinguishing marks, but inevitably there will be an institutional push-back. 'But what about the other things we have to deliver on? We still have to do this, and that...'

To be distinctive you have to go after that difference wholeheartedly, otherwise you won't be able to amplify it enough for your consumers to notice it. And in order to do that, you have to stop going after a bunch of other stuff. Our solution, by the way, is not to suddenly reinvent yourself, but to aim at three to five elements that, over the next three years, you plan to invest in and do incredibly well – and own in the minds of your customers.

Key takeaways

- All businesses want their services to be distinctive, but that's not enough; the distinctiveness must point to what is quintessentially of the brand. And today, your customer experience journey, rather than your brand, is the shortcut to how customers view what you offer. Your customer experience, therefore, is your brand.

- You can make your service distinctive by:
  - on one level, translating your brand values into how your service looks and behaves;
  - on a further level, identifying your brand's 'hallmark' experiences and embedding them into a service that delivers them as points of distinction successfully for your customers. This involves creating tangible proof points for your customers.

- What a brand *says* is marketing; what it *does* is its service proposition. To develop your service proposition requires a central idea based on the main benefit your service offers, a set of statements that support this, and the proof points you intend to offer that back it up from your customers' perspectives. You can use a Vision Wheel to help develop this thinking.

- Creating a truly distinctive service is hard, because it's easy to confuse your brand proposition with your service proposition. This can lead to disagreement internally. It also involves understanding what you're good at as an organization (and what you're not), and being prepared to drop elements that don't contribute positively to your service distinctiveness. These can be uncomfortable to face up to.

The challenge of change 06

Now you've taken the time to understand the full range of hurdles to overcome when transforming your customer experience, you'll be in an excellent position to share these insights with your colleagues. Many of them will value learning more about the common challenges you face, so you can all get to work on them without delay. However, you might also be feeling a little daunted, and we don't blame you. There's no need to worry, though; there are solutions to these problems in Part Two.

First let's recap the six challenges. To start, we looked at what goes wrong when you don't have an outside-in view of your customer experience. All sorts of disjointed customer approaches emanate from this, including creating duplicated, unhelpful and inconsistent services. This can be exacerbated by the siloed structure of organizations, which means the all-important, horizontally focused activities are hard to mobilize.

Next we examined the various barriers to creating a powerful and inspiring vision of the customer experience. These include confusion about what a vision actually is, difficulties with 'seeing' the end result, and a lack of accountability in translating the vision into reality – all of which lead to creating a vision that just isn't compelling enough. The vision gets watered down, peters out, and doesn't end up achieving what it could.

We also asked questions about why businesses find it hard to work at dual speeds when implementing new ideas around services. Agile and longer-term, vision-led thinking are activities with different metabolic rates; this can give your business health problems, especially in a heavily personnel-based service culture that takes time to change. There are solutions to this, but many organizations struggle to implement them, as this friction has its roots in how people from their own professional backgrounds are motivated to work in different ways.

At this point, we moved on to the topic of emotion in your customer experience – where did it go? Customers buy because of feelings, not logic, so embedding emotion into services is essential. This is difficult because of the challenges associated with quantifying and predicting emotional reactions, which make it hard for you to justify spending money on them. There's also the issue of the amount of time it takes to encourage customers to feel emotionally about a service that may have been price- or function-led for years. The result is that your business doesn't take emotion as seriously as it could.

And finally, we explored the challenge of making your service distinctive so it comes across as intrinsically 'yours'. The opinion your customers have of your brand is created by the experience they have of your service – they're one and the same. So you need a proposition that both encapsulates all the elements of your service and makes it from you alone. There are a number of difficulties with achieving this, including understanding what a branded service proposition is in the first place, and agreeing what the service values should be. You need there to be a high degree of self-awareness across your business, as well as a willingness to face uncomfortable truths about what you are to your customers, versus what you say you are.

Your organizational structure might be working against you

It won't have escaped your notice that many of the challenges we outlined above have their foundations in the way large organizations are structured. They're not set up around their customers, but around their own internal functions; the presence of a customer service department or a customer experience manager unfortunately doesn't negate this. Even small businesses are arranged to serve their own needs first, although their internal communications are more straightforward. Very hierarchical structures can also make it difficult for your organization to innovate. When everyone further up the tree has to approve budgets for any level of change, experimentation can easily fizzle out. The end result of these silos, hierarchies and political trenches is that the infrastructure and mechanisms for getting more of the right services to market faster can feel grindingly slow.

Of course, there's nothing wrong with your company being big; size is one indicator of success. The problem comes when business growth leads to a lack of awareness of, and focus on, your customers' experience at every touchpoint. How your organization decides to deal with this central challenge is critical to what your customers end up thinking and feeling about your brand, and therefore how many of them choose to buy from you.

In case you imagine we're suggesting you institute some kind of corporate makeover, you can relax. Of course you can't change the structure of your business; apart from anything else, there are plenty of good reasons why it's set up the way it is. But you can find ways of making its structure work in your favour by using design thinking and tools to inspire and facilitate change. And it's the competencies of design-led change that we'll be explaining to you in Part Two. Your company may have something of an 'old school' approach to change, but our own experiences and skills will help you tap into more contemporary views on how to make things happen.

In this chapter we highlight factors that are discussed in most modern change management playbooks. They resonate with us because they are particularly important when the change is necessitated by the redesign or innovation of new services and customer experiences. We also borrow a model from two experts in 'positive organization psychology' to observe how the kinds of behaviours they advocate when it comes to getting organizations to change match exactly the ways that we as Designers work with our clients.

Just can't find the time

This is probably the toughest of all barriers to overcome (assuming your leadership is bought in and you have permission to work differently). There is always something more urgent to attend to. In work, as in life, prioritization is a continual activity and there are no easy solutions. What we would say, though, is that time spent designing and prototyping the right propositions and services is time well spent if the alternative results in the wrong product in the market or underwhelming delivery. And of course the process of designing – together – has itself other benefits for your organization and culture.

People don't feel accountable for their part of the total experience

Obvious perhaps, but the crucial point is that whereas an internal change, for example, a reorganization, merger or change of IT platform, can be managed department by department, delivering a significant change for customers needs to be well coordinated to ensure the service and customers' journeys feel joined-up and seamless.

Samantha from Transport for London describes the importance of accountability as the pace of design and delivery increases. Each part of the operation needs to do its bit:

Getting faster and smarter at reacting in as close to real time as possible to our customers' issues and ideas is critical to how we deliver quick wins whilst waiting for the strategic roadmap to play out. The 'plumbing' between every channel and every team needs to be right from a process point of view, but will only be successful if every person inside the business feels accountable for owning and improving the customer experience.

While at National Grid, Adam looked to hand over the vision to each business area as soon as he could to ensure that each area of the business was involved in generating their own customer-driven plans in response to the target experience we'd designed. He says, 'Each area has to own and shape their own plan'.

It's hard for people to let go of their departmental objectives and operate as one team

Services these days are omnichannel and customers expect businesses to be joined-up when it comes to managing customer relationships, so making new products, services and experience happen requires a strong sense of a dedicated team. The management challenge is that although this makes sense, organizations don't make it easy for their people to work as one. Objectives, the internal market for resources, different approaches to initiating and managing projects and so on can stand in the way. Samantha from Transport for London says that design methods and the project structure of 'the design process' provide a great platform for collaboration:

A 'one team ethos' with common objectives and incentives which means everyone pulls together around the delivery of a shared design and plan. The beauty of the design-led approach is how collaboratively consensus is achieved across a multifunctional team – all the right people are already passionate and clear about what they need to do when it's time to build and deliver the changes.

We believe that a customer-driven and design-led project is a powerful tool because it puts everybody (including your frontline colleagues and your customers) on a level playing field and it places the customer and their needs at the centre (rather than the needs of any one function).

The organization isn't committed

It's hard to put any firm numbers on it but an intuitive estimate is that it takes three years to move an organization from one that is inherently product-focused in its approaches to one that is customer-driven. Having been involved in this change and led our part of it by designing new things with these organizations, it is clear to us that there are factors that help support this change. Of course there needs to be leadership from the top of the organization. There needs to be a clear vision for the business that is told not through the commercials but through customers' stories from the future. As we'll go on to discuss in the next chapter, the vision needs to be both aspirational and pragmatic and it must feel achievable. Then, a critical mass of people have to have had a tangible experience, through projects, of working in a very different way, using insight on customers in a different way – and seeing a very different outcome.

Keith from E.ON Energy mentions one other really important factor, discipline:

> *A culture of customer-centred performance management is evolving. Many more of the conversations we're having about the performance of the service and the business are customer-driven. This transformation has happened because of a continual focus on delivering our customer experience principles that define, for E.ON, what a great service and experience is – and on disciplined measurement and reporting of the single outcome measurement of Net Promoter. And it's clear to the business that this is working.*

A fresh approach to change that resonates with the world of Design

Change is a complicated animal. Some people hate it while others thrive on it, but one thing's for certain: large companies have always found it problematic. As a way of tackling this, organizational psychologists are starting to challenge traditional attitudes to change. Instead of asking people to accept and try to adapt to it, they're helping employees to shift their beliefs about what's possible. This means it feels like the change comes from the inside rather than being imposed from the outside. It's an approach that acts like a bridge between the challenges we've looked at so far and the change we'd like to see – a change, as it happens, that our design-led approach to getting more to market fully supports.

So how does this work? It's a complex area outside the scope of this book, but outlining it here will help you to see the link between what you can do to effect transformational change, and the way outside-in thinking creates the best services for your customers. Let's look at one framework that doesn't mention 'design' directly, yet seems to describe perfectly what Designers, design thinking and design tools bring to the challenge of transforming services and the customer experience.

In their paper, 'Change the way you lead change' (Quinn and Wellman, 2013), the authors set out an approach to leading change inside organizations based on their research in positive organization psychology. On reading the paper it struck us how much the 'positive change' statements were supportive of what we understand to be the role of design methods. Design-led projects are inherently creative, optimistic and collaborative in their approach. We often describe 'designing' as a format for collaborative planning. The effects of using design tools, defining an optimistic vision and making it tangible quickly through prototyping give the to-market process and the change underlying it a boost of speed.

Below are the main elements of the 'positive organizational change' approach set out by the paper's authors. While reading this list, have a think about your organization. Does it feel like one capable of positive organizational change? If you were in charge (which you might be), what tools and initiatives would you champion in order to become an organization that's able to make more good things happen for your customers?

What positive organizational change looks like (and how much this suggests a role for design thinking and tools)

- **New thinking and ideas can come from anybody in the organization**
  The initiative to drive positive change within an organization can come from any level of the business. Staff are inspired to bring evidence-based ideas to the attention of senior management with a view to getting change projects underway.

- **Processes are designed to empower, not constrain**
  The culture of the organization is receptive to change. Managers who can identify and create processes that help the organization to adapt in an effective way are valued. An ability to craft efficient processes that empower a 'living business', able to respond to many constantly changing elements, is prized. To fuel this constant change, teams adopt working methods that are energizing and collaborative.

- **Learning through doing, not just learning through data**
  The process of being a living business involves a greater level of perceived instability as the systems, processes and relationships are more dynamic. The emphasis has shifted away from a controlled, linear approach to one of continuous learning in real time through prototyping and testing to find new ideas.

Notions of learning through doing and recognition that game-changing ideas can come from anywhere in the organization are central to the way we approach projects with our clients.

- **Stories about the future state of the business, not just historical performance**
  Communication about where the organization is today is supplemented with communication about its desired future, which we call in this book a 'compelling vision'. Conversations incorporate what the organization is working towards through a lens of what is most valued by itself *and* those that it serves. This thorough view becomes the guiding vision that everybody across the business can own and get behind.

When we work with our clients in workshop to explore their service and operation and imagine new solutions, we're doing with them what academics would identify as 'appreciative inquiry', the objective being to transport people (in their minds) to an imagined positive and improved state for their business and customers by asking questions about what is most valued and what is most desired. The resulting images become the envisioned system with which we and they can start planning and reorganizing.

- **Errors and exceptions are seen as a source of inspiration and learning**
  Organizations seek variance. Failures as well as positive deviance are valued as constructive so that 'problems' by their nature no longer exist, only 'opportunities'. Positive patterns are expanded. Examples of disruption from other companies are used as inspiration for change. Frontline staff who 'go the extra mile' are role models not rule breakers.

- **Optimism and vision**
  The organization has a positive working culture filled with exploration and experimentation. It savours experiences, includes play and has a forum for integrating new views or approaches that will shape its future.

Bringing all these elements together is the best way of creating a powerful vision, which then gets translated into effective and energetic action. It's no small task, but if your business is to move away from the traditional approach of expertise being the dominant force, to learning through doing, sketching out ideas, prototyping, and then developing them, it's essential. You can't achieve all this on your own, but you can start to take a fresh look at your own attitude to change. Seeing it as something you 'are' rather than something you 'do' is a great first step.

Helen from Dubai Airports describes how the team realized that having the vision set out and agreed wouldn't be enough. They needed to work differently and put in place structures and mechanisms to keep the vision alive while working towards delivering it:

> Once we'd recognized we needed to take more direct ownership of the quality of the customer experience, it became clear that new capabilities and ways of working were required. It wasn't enough to have a vision; we needed to put in place what was needed to make it a reality.
>
> We had to re-imagine how the organization worked. Customer experience had to become the concern of the whole organization, not solely those engaged in face-to-face customer service, with the mantra 'you are either directly serving a passenger or serving someone who is'.
>
> The organization now has monthly Experience and Business boards and eight cross-disciplinary 'Labs'. The Labs are strategic working groups aimed at realizing the vision through guiding existing projects and activities, as well as conceiving new projects aimed at enhancing the customer experience today. Sessions are led and facilitated by some of the most senior members of the organization and aimed at driving the business forward with the customer experience at its heart. Objectives for projects are borne of customer functional and/or emotional needs, identified by the organization's research activities.
>
> Action plans to deliver these objectives are curated to ensure solutions are responsive to needs. Benefits are defined and evaluated throughout the project lifecycle to ensure value is being derived for the customer, the organization and the people working within it. This cross-pollination of ideas and people has begun to permeate business-as-usual, with frontline operations people working alongside service designers and project specialists to deliver experiences that work functionally but with an even higher level of service quality.
>
> We've recognized we're on a journey and to expect successes and failures on the way, but importantly we understood that we had to change ourselves to positively impact our customers.

Key takeaways

- Service transformation necessitates organizational change, not necessarily in a structural sense, but in terms of attitudes across your business. This creates the challenge of how to harness all areas of the business to focus on your customers, so the experience they have of your service is positive.

- It takes time to develop well-designed services, but it's vital to allocate that time because it has a long-term benefit.

- Different areas of your business need to work together to effect change, but the individuals within them may not feel accountable for their part of the process. This is often exacerbated by the way organizations are set up – they don't encourage working as one, in service of the customer. This can lead to inconsistent results.

- Given it tends to take three years to move from a product-focused organization to one that's customer-driven, businesses need to have an extraordinary commitment to the process of change.

- It takes time and resources to help employees shift their beliefs about what's possible and to change how they work. We can look to the field of 'positive organizational psychology' to help us interpret why design thinking and tools seem to offer one approach to challenging and changing people's beliefs about how a service can be designed and delivered.

Reference

Quinn, R E and Wellman, N (2013) 'Change the way you lead change', Stephen M Ross School of Business, University of Michigan, Executive White Paper Series

PART TWO
The skills

Let's revisit what you're trying to achieve: better services in your organization, resulting in a transformed experience for your customers. In Part One we helped you understand why this can be so difficult and, in doing so, highlighted the skills and approaches to focus on in order to make your service a success. It probably felt like a tall order. So enough of the challenges now – you want to know what to do about them. How do you get past all the problems we've just talked about, so you can create new services your customers will love and your company will appreciate?

There are seven things you need to be good at in order to bring more of the right services to market faster, and learning them is a bit like exercising new muscles. Practising some of the elements will feel a bit alien to you – even painful – and after a while you may start to wonder if you should carry on. Please do. Even if you only pick up a couple of new skills from this part of the book, you'll be streets ahead of most others in your organization.

The best way to express these seven areas is as a wheel. That's because, although we present them here in a certain order, they all need to be constantly in your mind. As you read Part Two, you'll see how one feeds off and contributes to the others all the way through your service transformation project. These seven skills can also be viewed as seven outcomes. If you can get them right, you'll get closer to achieving the results you want for your project and get more of the right services to market faster.

Figure P2.1   Seven skills for you and your teams to master that will help you get more of the right services and customer experiences to market faster

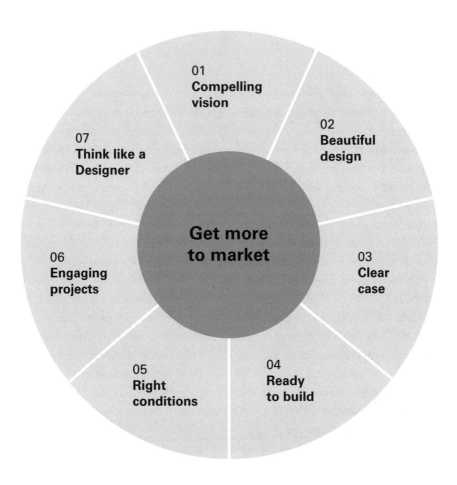

Create a
compelling vision

Just wanting to transform your customer experience, no matter how strongly you feel about it, is never enough. You need to bring your colleagues along with you, motivating large numbers of people to stop doing what they feel comfortable with and start doing bold and novel things instead. To achieve this, you need to surface one strong, exciting and motivating idea that everyone can own, and that you can achieve within the next three to five years: you need a compelling vision.

This is important, because not only is it the vehicle for your whole service transformation, it's also the element that will give you the biggest return on your investment. Of 474 executives surveyed for a *Harvard Business Review* article (Harvard Business Review Analytic Services, 2015), 89 per cent said a strong sense of collective purpose drives employee satisfaction, 84 per cent said it can affect an organization's ability to transform, and 80 per cent said it helps increase customer loyalty. In other words, a business that solely focuses on maximizing sales and minimizing costs can only get so far, because this alone is not motivating enough for its customers or for those working in it.

What's more, when you work in a complex organization, no single person can ever hold the complete picture of what a new service and experience will look like – everyone has their own version. That doesn't mean to say there aren't ideas aplenty (that can be part of the problem!) but this is exactly why you need that central ambition, an ambition that's vivid enough to drive change forward. How else can you get everyone behind it?

As we mentioned in Chapter 2, one of the problems you and your colleagues will face is creating a clear understanding of what a vision is. Often, what an organization calls its vision is in fact a set of corporate and commercial objectives. These lack the tangibility so essential to a compelling vision. A vision is something you can 'see'; it's the depiction of the future state you want to design. And because the notions of 'vision' and 'objective' are used interchangeably by many companies, you'll need to position your vision carefully; people need more than objectives to get excited about change. In fact, the best visions package up and give legitimacy to what your colleagues are already thinking on their own, but haven't yet been able to make a collective mental shift towards.

A good analogy for the vision as a package of compelling elements is to think of a LEGO® set. It comes in a box with a colourful picture on the front depicting what your design will look like when it's finished; this is the equivalent of the 'future state' of your transformed service. On the back are some pictures showing the major, playable points of the kit; these make it seem tangible and exciting, as if it's really going to happen. Inside the box, it gets more detailed. The instruction book contains the list of parts you'll need to create your model (in other words, make your vision a reality) and of course the actual instructions, which provide a plan of action.

When we work with businesses to set their vision, we have the advantage of coming from the outside – this makes it easier to listen, draw out the beginnings of a bold idea, and build a consensus. Our aim here is to give you the tools to create that objectivity for yourself, so you can lead your internal stakeholders through an engaging and creative process. This pulls everyone together. And doing so is a kind of release – 'Yes! That's it, that's what we've been trying to articulate!'

By the end of this chapter you'll be able to create your own compelling vision as the first step in your customer experience transformation journey. In doing so, you'll start to see the concept of a vision in a whole new way.

But first, why is a compelling, actionable vision so essential?

- It helps you make better decisions.
- It motivates your colleagues.

A compelling vision for your service gives your decision-making a strong purpose

What's the difference between where you are now and where you want to be? Having an answer to this question enables you to accurately assess your current operations and plans for change, and to put forward clear recommendations for the future. It means your leaders can define a roadmap so they can plan projects, resources, partnerships and investments, ahead of time. Once these are in place, you'll find it easier to make those difficult decisions about what to stop doing, what to start doing, and what to continue with. You'll find investing in the development of a vision enhances the quality of the rest of your investment choices.

If your business is like most, you'll be focusing the majority of your efforts day to day on fixes and tactical activity. Much as you'd love to have more time to 'think big', it rarely seems to happen. But when you have a vision for the customer experience, you automatically gain a more strategic set of requirements and actions. And when you apply these to assess the customer initiatives already in place, their value or lack of value to the business will become clear. A compelling vision also helps you avoid investing time and resources in insignificant, reactive and incremental projects in favour of long-term and meaningful transformation. Without it, teams across your business may only be able to move forward with smaller pots of money and deliver superficial change. With your compelling vision, however, you can make the case for transformational levels of investment.

Finally, having a three- to five-year vision means you can future-proof any investment you're making in your IT infrastructure. Without this approach, there's a risk your new technology will turn into the very constraint you're spending money to remove.

Since privatization, over 20 individual operators manage the UK rail industry's relationship with rail customers. That makes sense until you remember that significant parts of the customer journey, often the most important parts, are delivered by other parts of the industry. Moreover, for customers making journeys with more than one operating company, the experience can be inconsistent.

One of the Rail Delivery Group's responsibilities is to deliver whole-network solutions for the train operating companies and for travelling customers. One of the really important responsibilities is customer information and communication. With the rail network run by 28 individual companies, providing information to customers, especially at times of disruption, is a vital part of making the whole network work for customers. Crispin Humm explained the challenge:

When we asked Engine to help us develop a vision and a roadmap, from which we could make significant changes to the experience of customer information and communication, we knew we needed to adopt a customer-centred method – but we also knew doing so would be a challenge to our organizations. When the industry came together in meetings and then in design workshops to tackle these particular issues, the industry group really struggled to have a coherent view.

The creation of a customer-centred vision, a 'North Star' for the industry, was a real watershed moment. This vision for 'what the emerging customer wants and will expect' has helped the industry group to focus, prioritize, exercise control when in dialogue with powerful stakeholders, and communicate.

The rail industry is unique in as much as the industry itself must buy in to a vision and programme for change, and then the individual operators must sign up too. If the vision and change plan had been created centrally by us behind closed doors then the change challenge, I think, would be enormous. However, the design approach is all about collaboration and co-creation. The outputs are therefore informed by the customer and shaped by the individual businesses that will be implementing key parts of the change.

A compelling vision motivates people

Most change fails due to resistance from employees and a lack of support from managers, so the emotional connection a strong vision creates is essential. After all, it's people who create change, and they need to feel motivated to do it. Having a vision 'inspires employee engagement, fosters customer engagement, and helps boost company performance – among other benefits' (Harter *et al*, 2013). This is highly valuable as 'engaged employees produce better business outcomes than do other employees across industry, across company size and nationality, and in good economic times and bad' (Gallup, 2017). Unfortunately, many organizations focus more on training their front-line staff on the technical aspects of a new solution than on helping them see the value in making a positive move forward. Even senior stakeholders need to feel motivated by having a significant idea to latch onto, with the evidence and a concrete plan to back it up. People must feel part of the change.

PegasusLife builds accommodation for older people and, although their core business is property, their customers see them as providing assisted living services to them in their homes. When we started working with PegasusLife, we learned that selling retirement properties can be difficult. Many potential customers are reticent; it's not easy discussing and planning what might be your last home. In addition, many of the properties being sold have not yet been built, so sales teams are asking prospective owners to buy off plan. It's increasingly the services and level of service that drive a customer's decision to buy from Pegasus instead of a competitor. Clare reflects on the role the service vision and the target customer experience played in helping the team at PegasusLife imagine and develop a better purchase and ownership experience for the residents of their properties:

It's very difficult to get people to 'see' the future before it exists, especially when the current offering is so ingrained in customers' minds, and the current offering is so stigmatized. We had to get the internal sales team seeing and believing the future – they couldn't bring the proposition to life for customers if they didn't believe it themselves. Two aspects of our project with Engine worked well and have really stuck.

Firstly, creating the right environment for customer-facing teams to 'design the future' through workshops that gave them a platform to explore what hinders them in today's world, but also their vision for the service we should provide and the business we need to become.

And secondly, creating outputs from the workshops that teams saw as refreshing and different. Describing the experience 'today' and the experience we want to create 'tomorrow' made it super-easy for teams to grasp the vision. They recognized the descriptions of the past and were able to visualize the energy and the art of the possible. We could all see clear water between the service we wanted to build and today's reality; this gave people a strong sense that they needed to act.

What makes your vision compelling?

We know having a plain old vision isn't enough – it has to be a compelling one. But what distinguishes a 'regular' vision from one that will inspire and motivate everyone involved? There are three elements to this, and each one requires its own knowledge, skills and tools to put it into practice.

You know you've got a motivating vision when:

1 you have a strong, central idea that feels right, is simple, and captures the imagination;

2 you've discovered enough customer insight and evidence to make your vision robust;

3 your vision embodies a story about your company, customers or the world you operate in that is easy to tell and re-tell.

We'll go through each in turn.

A strong, central idea that feels right, is simple and captures the imagination

You want everyone in your business to see your vision as smoking hot. One thing that makes a vision compelling is when it can be traced back to a key insight your business has about its customers or its industry (ideally both). To come up with this idea you need to spot a win-win benefit: one your customers will value and your colleagues will get excited about.

So what happens if you don't have a compelling vision to motivate change? Most likely, your transformation will end up being driven by a need to fix what's not working. A rolling programme of fixes and incremental improvements will be welcomed by your customers, but may not significantly increase their loyalty to you, or your company's competitiveness. Without a clear vision, effort can be expended by many people with little return. We've worked in organizations in which it's felt as though many well-intentioned people were battling each other for ownership of the customer experience. Samantha from Transport for London describes what can happen if the organization doesn't have a clear vision for service:

You end up with some good work on paper but very little actually out there for customers to buy and experience. What does make it to market will often be of limited value and limited lifespan because of its lack of integration. This can be dangerously costly to the organization and sends all the wrong signals to the customer.

A compelling vision, on the other hand, is one that inspires everyone to believe it's worth the effort, and that it's achievable. Let's look at an example of how compelling vision for service was used to catalyse change in one organization we know well.

When we first started working with Helsinki Airport, it looked, felt and operated like most other northern European city airports. And like them, it also faced stiff competition for routes and passengers. We wanted to make it stand out in its corner of Europe, so we developed a strong, central idea that captured the qualities of the city and the region in a way that could be translated into their service design. This helped us gain the buy-in of their CEO and senior management, and when we'd got them on board, we used it to define a whole new approach to delivering their customer experience through a range of services. This central vision was based on what we termed 'Nordic Wonder' and had four qualities: 'perfect essentials' (the removal of complication to make the experience of their services hassle-free for travellers); 'joined-up' (giving a personalized and proactive experience); 'naturally nurtured' (helping their customers feel better than when they arrived, by bringing the outdoors in and creating a sense of freshness and tranquillity); and 'Nordic experience' (a celebration of the seasonal diversity of the country's landscape and culture).

These aspects of the vision then became practical applications. For example, the elements of relaxation and control were brought to life by enabling travellers to pre-order service packages to enjoy once they got there, and to take advantage of not having to transfer their hand baggage between flights. The result was the airport's customers having more time to relax, browse, and spend money, as they felt confident and in control of their journeys. This meant they felt better in mind, body and soul and had tasted something quintessentially Finnish. As old terminal buildings are demolished and new ones built in their place, the vision is to blend natural landscaping with the steel and glass and blur the threshold between the inside and outside. In this way, customers can feel part of an environment and experience that is 'naturally nurtured', again an important aspect of Finnish life and culture. And Johanna's favourites: 'I especially liked the ideas that were surprising and delightful. We built the Winter Wonderland for Christmas. We've brought Nordic snow into the airport.'

You can see that framing a compelling vision for your service involves homing in on a strong, central idea that resonates with your people, excites their imagination, anticipates the solutions you'll need to come up with, and is a response to the strategic direction set by your business.

Backed up by enough insight and evidence to make your vision robust

Like any organization, yours will already have an abundance of research for you to draw upon. This is a good thing, because you'll need evidence to prove your vision is heading your business in a valuable direction. Ideally this research will inform you about your customers and your marketplace, as both are essential to support your idea.

The problem with research is there's so much of it, which makes it difficult to unearth what you need. However, cutting through the clutter of data is essential for spotting some truths about where your customers, your company and your world are going. The process can feel like more of an art than a science; you're viewing these documents with your imagination switched on. What are the implications of the data for your customers and business? What would you envision if you took the available trend data and extrapolated it to an extreme? What would your competitors do, faced with the same information?

Once you've identified the research elements that back up your vision, you can support your argument with tangible and intangible benefits to your business that can be realized through implementing your central idea.

So, if we take the fictional example of an airport in Table 7.1, we can trace the logic of how investing in the experience in specific ways drives business benefits and takes you closer to your vision. Tracing the logic in this way provides a framework against which to find or estimate the numbers that will form your business case.

Table 7.1 Tracing the logic of tangible investment in the experience to benefits to the business

Tangible investment in the experience	Direct customer benefit	Customer outcome	Business benefit	Delivery against our vision 'Preparing you for your journey'
Tailored, timely and relevant information delivered direct to passengers' mobile phones.	Customers are more aware of the time they have available to them before their flight.	Few customers are late to the gate. And more customers feel relaxed and comfortable, spending more time in the Departure Lounge.	Fewer departures are delayed, which reduces charges and penalties for airlines and the airport. Increased revenue from Departure Lounges.	Passengers arrive in their aircraft seats less stressed and more contented.

Centred around a great story that is easy to tell and re-tell

Have you ever wondered what makes something go viral? Often it's that there's a story that is emotionally engaging enough to be understood, appreciated and told over and over again; it strikes a universal cord.

Early in our work with Dubai Airports, we ran a large event and invited the CEO to rally his management teams around the transformational vision we'd begun to form together. Over two days, we involved them in testing and building on our initial thinking, and we encouraged them to take their experience back to their teams to get the conversation going. We knew, however, that it would take effort to maintain the excitement and momentum of the initial vision and of the event. It would take consistency and energy, so much so that it couldn't be the responsibility of one team alone. So, we identified what we call a 'hero project'. This is an initiative that's short-term enough to demonstrate early on what the larger vision is aiming to achieve, but is significant enough to do more than fix the basics. For the airport, our hero project was to focus on the culture and training of front-line staff in the terminals, redesigning the approach it took to training. After proving the validity in a pilot with 300 staff, we began a programme to retrain the rest. This meant we could speak to over 1,500 people about the new vision and direction for the airport.

Do you have the narrative, the arguments and the collateral to get every-one else excited about your vision? Once you've formulated your vision into a story, you'll find it easier to convince people internally. This story should come in several sizes, each suitable for different audiences and occasions: a one-sentence sound bite, a longer story, and a full presentation.

How to create a compelling vision

So, you know the qualities your vision must possess in order to be compel-ling, but it can feel overwhelming. There are so many elements to put into place, and you're not sure if you have the skills for them all. This next part of the chapter will break down what needs to be done so it becomes clearer.

There are six main areas to focus on when you're creating a compelling vision:

- doing your research and getting your facts straight;
- gaining a deep understanding of your customers;
- working from the future backwards;
- enabling your colleagues to feel they own the vision;
- bringing your vision to life;
- creating a plan.

Let's look at them in more detail.

Do your research

A brilliant vision is one that understands what's right for your business, your customers, your colleagues and your brand. It can't just be a rewrite of your existing corporate vision, mission and values; rather, it describes where you think your company needs to be at some point in the future. It must repre-sent a clear and actionable proposition that will motivate your colleagues to act and direct the experiences you want your customers to have.

This means you being informed and having fresh insight and ideas. To achieve this, work with four inputs that shape a service vision together:

- an understanding of your customers and their worlds;
- an understanding of your business, services, capabilities and operating model;
- an understanding of your brand positioning and values;
- a view on the future operating environment that your vision is a response to.

In our experience, the area usually needing the most work is that of building a clear and rich picture of the customers your transformed service will serve. This is because, for most organizations, it's the one area of understanding that's least developed. Bear in mind, as well, that these customers may not necessarily be the same as the ones you have today.

Start with your customers

Most businesses have a plethora of customer data and research. Few, however, believe they really understand who their customers are, what they need, the attitudes and expectations they bring, and the reality of how customers use their service. I'm sure you already have customer segmentations that tell you who buys what, and inform your product development and marketing. But what they don't tend to reveal are the needs and preferences underlying your customers' decisions, nor do they shed much light on the nature of the relationships they want to have with you. Relying on customer sales and marketing data can lead you to closed insights, which encourage you to focus simply on improving your existing sales and marketing processes. Without a more qualitative understanding, and the licence to apply your imagination, you'll find it hard to hone in on what your customers will value even more than what you currently offer, or indeed what they will value three years from now.

One driver for defining a compelling vision is to hit upon something that, running ahead, you could imagine 'pitching' to a room full of your customers (not to your board) and getting them excited about it. To achieve this, you need to know enough about what they value. Annoyingly, the way to find this out isn't usually to go and ask them! Your vision is a tool to drive innovation, but your customers aren't great at telling you what they're going to like at some point in the future. Informed by your customer research, and also through exploring what's going on in the world of services around you, you need to apply some imagination.

Work from the future backwards

Your analysis of your market and macroeconomic environment, your knowledge of the capabilities and investment potential of your business, your competitive benchmarking, your review of the technology landscape, and your commercial target-setting have all been central to setting out your vision. And so they should be. But these types of analysis tend to produce high-level objectives, rather than what you've now learned is an envisioned vision. At best they describe the future 'why', not the future 'what' or 'how'. They're certainly not a vision in themselves.

For instance, you might discover a new competitor is about to enter your marketplace, with a superior technology offering to your own. You also know your customers value a slick digital experience, so this leads you to think a re-vamp of your technology and website must be essential. However, this isn't really a vision, it's a set of reasons for change. To 'envision' means something different and specific. The best way to create your vision is not to start with your macro context, but to visualize the experience that will be of most value, both to your customers and your business, three to five years from now. This imagined future state becomes your vision, which then becomes your objective, which then becomes your strategy to deliver. This is, in essence, what design-led change is about.

Build your vision together

It's not only your colleagues at the top of your organization that you have to listen to, but also the ones beside and below you. Your job is to hear their voices and create a collective understanding about what your business needs to do. Rallying people around your vision, and making sure they feel a degree of ownership of it, means they'll feel invested in its success. The trick is to describe the change your business knows in its heart it needs to make, in a way that encapsulates what you know your customers will love as well.

Remember, resist pressure simply to restate the corporate aspiration or brand values using different words, instead of a vision for a new service that people will want to buy. If you can imagine selling your vision to a 'real' customer, not to a shareholder, you've passed this test.

Bring your vision to life

Remember in Chapter 2 we talked about how it can be hard for people to 'see' your vision? Try asking your graphic designers or creative marketing agencies you work with to help you visualize these changes so people can get a handle on what they will look like in reality. You can do this through storyboards that tell the story of how your customers will use your service in the future, or through mocked-up customer communications (sometimes called 'adcepts'). You could even make a simple movie telling the story or vision through your customers' eyes.

Why not build prototypes your colleagues can play with? This is easy in digital, but we also use LEGO® to represent how customers and frontline staff will interact with a service – it makes it real. We've built full-size prototypes too, using foam board, actors and furniture, to show how elements of a service will work in airports and retail environments.

Figure 7.1   Much can be learned by building full-sized prototypes quickly and from cheap materials. We borrowed an empty car dealership for four weeks to role-play customer service and define interior features and requirements for technology

Figure 7.2   If you can't prototype services at full-scale, use LEGO® or Playmobil® figures, cardboard and glue to build your service desktop-sized. Work with your customers and frontline colleagues to explore how your service could work

Create a plan

Your service strategy isn't only a compelling and robust vision, it needs a plan as well. Your vision will excite everyone but your plan makes it feel achievable, which in turn makes your vision even more enticing. Of course, at the vision stage you won't have a detailed set of actions mapped out, but you should have some idea of how you're going to achieve what you need to do. Most of these changes should be long-term and transformational, but some must be more immediate so people can see results quickly. We'll discuss the importance of providing enough detail and of planning in Chapter 10.

Here are five questions to test the strength of your vision:

- **A strong, central idea:** do you have one?

- **Insight and evidence:** do you have any?

- **Excitement:** are your colleagues showing enthusiasm about your vision?

- **Clear and communicable by others:** is your vision spreading virally at a senior level?

- **Momentum:** is your vision unblocking concerns and gaining resource allocation?

Key takeaways

- Having a compelling vision for your service is essential, because it brings all parts of the business together and gives your decision-making a strong purpose.

- It's also important for encouraging bigger-picture and longer-term thinking. Without a vision, you're likely to descend into day-to-day tactical fixes, which don't give you the value of a larger-scale transformation.

- With a vision, people feel engaged and motivated. It's important to focus on this rather than simply on training frontline staff to deliver new solutions.

- You know your vision is compelling enough when:

  - You have a central idea that links directly to a key insight about what your customers value, and that your colleagues can get excited about. This discourages your organization from only fixing what's not working today.

  - You know enough about your service, and your competitors, to back your vision up with facts.

  - You can create a story about it that is easy to tell and re-tell, allowing your vision to travel around your organization without being diluted.

- Creating a compelling vision involves:

  - researching your customers and their worlds, so you understand what's right for them and your brand – this will usually mean fresh research, giving you new insights;

  - visualizing what your customers will want in three to five years, and planning back from there;

  - collaborating with and inspiring your colleagues to rally people around it;

  - creating an achievable plan that feels realistic.

References

Gallup (2017) State of the global workplace, Gallup Press

Harter, J K, Schmidt, F L, Agrawal, S and Plowman, S K (2013) The relationship between engagement at work and organizational outcomes: 2012 Q12® Meta-analysis, Gallup Research

Harvard Business Review Analytic Services (2015) The business case for purpose, *Harvard Business Review*, Harvard Business School Publishing

Design your service beautifully

08

When you think about what 'beautiful design' means to you, a physical product probably comes to mind. It might be your iPhone, the classic Jaguar F-Type, a Nest thermostat, a Danish-designed chair from the 1950s, those amazing spectacles that allow you to adjust the lenses until they focus, or even Concorde. It works not just because it looks beautiful, is easy to use, or solves your problem elegantly; it's because it does all three at the same time. A superb piece of design makes you *feel good* when you're using it.

Although we can all point to products we consider to be beautifully designed, it can feel like a leap to apply this thinking to a service. But why should it? A well-designed service also brings those three elements together, with an eye to how your customers will feel when they use it.

Naturally your service doesn't exist for its own sake – its purpose is to create value for your customers, thereby adding value to your business. The first element of value is the commercial advantage you will gain in your market by launching a great service, at least for a period. When you develop an initiative around something your competitors aren't doing, or that exceeds your customers' expectations of your brand and industry, you gain the ability to acquire new customers, reduce the number that leave you, and retain them for longer.

The UK's NatWest Bank enabled their customers to make emergency cash withdrawals from their ATMs if they lost their bank card, a service that was innovative and solved a genuine problem. The fact that few people were likely to use it wasn't the point; it was that it gave them something positive to talk about in their marketing that was different from other banks – and it was more than just marketing. Even if their competitors had wanted to copy the move, they couldn't have marketed it, because NatWest had already played that card.

In this chapter we'll look at why elegant and integrated design is essential for successful services, what makes a service 'beautiful', and how you can design your own services that will appeal to your customers in a powerful way. We'll set out attributes that, beyond the obvious ones, we think make for a beautifully designed service; qualities such as: originality, inclusivity, fitness for purpose and being right for the time and the culture it's operating in. We'll offer some tips for honing your ability to critique the services you use and develop a 'design language' so that you can inspire and direct others.

Why design beautifully?

Quite simply, because well-designed services are more successful in the market than those that aren't. People feel at ease when they use them, and as a result will choose them more frequently. Beautiful design connects emotionally with your customers, so it carries on working hard for you long after the experience is over for them.

Also, well-designed services cost less to operate. You might assume something of higher value to your customers must cost more for you to provide, but there's no reason why this should be the case. Beautifully designed physical products use materials efficiently, are reliable, and are so easy to use it's hard for customers to accidentally misuse them. The same applies to the design of services. An elegantly designed service is one that responds to both the needs of your customers and your business, creating maximum value for each by being easy to experience, delivered efficiently, and unlikely to cause customer and colleague errors.

Beautifully designed services are well thought through, they delight your customers by connecting emotionally with them, and they cost less (and cause fewer headaches) to implement than their poorly designed counterparts. Why wouldn't you want to design your services in this way? In fact, 'beautiful design' was probably what you had in mind all along, you just may not have had the language to describe it.

What makes a service beautifully designed?

Posing this question is a bit like asking what makes one office chair a design classic, selling at a premium for decades, while another is... well... just another office chair. Each does the same thing, but one does it beautifully. And that beauty isn't skin deep – it encapsulates something of real value that looks and works brilliantly and is, somehow, right for the moment. Every time you look at that chair you find yourself smiling; every time you sit on it you feel more relaxed and confident; every time someone asks where you got it from you feel a thrill of pride. And it's only a chair.

Johanna from Finnair defines beautiful service design as combining seamless operation with moments of delight:

> *I absolutely believe that services can be designed beautifully. We must strive for this. The industry is very good at copying. Copy paste, copy paste. But when you can make each element work together well you can get to beauty and this is hard to copy. When a service is designed well there are no distracting elements. It's well thought through and because of this it just works. Customers won't even know that it's been designed. And on top of this you can add elements of delight, the things people remember: 'I wouldn't have thought of that', 'I didn't think that was possible'. We are using technology more and more to achieve this. We can design-in positive surprises and cater for the things that people are not expecting. Experiences – even of an airport – can be beautiful in the sense that they can touch us emotionally.*

You'll gather from this that beautiful service design is one of those things that you recognize if you experience it, but that isn't always easy to define. There are, however, certain elements it always encapsulates, which we've done our best to explain here. In summary they are:

- emotional connection;
- originality;
- being of the moment;
- being about more than looks;
- detailed functionality;
- being designed for everyone;
- workability.

The experience connects emotionally

Pretty much all your services, in terms of their core functionality, pricing, and even the business processes your customers encounter along with them, can be copied by your competitors. What makes a service special is its ability to connect emotionally with your customers; this is the element that will keep them coming back for more. If you think back on the services you've found the most memorable, delightful and easy to use, you'll find the experience of participating in them will have left an emotional trace.

So what aspects of a service create most emotional connection? The place we buy it from can encourage us to feel a certain way, adding elements of exclusivity or reassurance in the case of financial products. The ability to personalize the experience helps us feel good about using it. If the service is delivered in an entertaining way it makes us feel excited and amused. Speed and reliability of delivery, when we complete transactions or give feedback, encourage us to feel a service is well built and is a respecter of our precious time; this in turn gives us a self-esteem boost, satisfied in the knowledge that we've made a smart choice of service provider.

In case you're wondering if it's possible to connect customers emotionally with even an extremely functional service, we can assure you it is. Take the pensions industry, for example. Traditionally, pensions have been sold and operated in a transactional way; any sales discussions around them focused purely on risk and fund performance. Providers also tended to assume customers were relatively wealthy and older, leading to clichéd depictions of golf courses and country clubs in their marketing material. Today, however, many more people are encouraged to have a pension (in the UK, everyone who is employed must have one). This means pension providers are having to work harder to make saving for retirement more relevant to young people and those on lower incomes, and to imagine more diverse social and life scenarios for their customers. They're not only having to communicate in a more emotional way to a less focused audience than before, but they're also designing and operating services that respond to the diversity of people's financial situations and images of themselves.

It's original (or has original ideas within it)

Novelty, or originality, is another essential element of a beautifully designed service. Newness is part of what people find attractive. We tend to stop noticing things if they don't change over time; it's part of the human condition to be fascinated by what stands out in a sea of sameness. We also like the occasional surprise in our relationships with our service providers.

When you're able to resolve stubborn customer pain-points in new ways, offer a clever solution to a problem or allow customers to interact in a new way, and your service looks and feels fresh and inspiring to use, people will talk about it. And your whole service doesn't need to be completely original; even if what's new is one detail, a behaviour or some fresh element of a feature, it can still get noticed.

Being original is not the same as creating a 'gimmick'. So the search for genuinely fresh adaptations to what you offer, which grab your customers' attention in ways that surprise, charm and genuinely benefit them, is continuous.

It's right for now

Have you ever experienced a new or improved service and thought, 'I wanted this all along but I just didn't know it?' That's because someone, somewhere, has figured out something about you – who you are, the situation you're in, the culture you inhabit – and made sure that service makes sense for you. We often talk to business people who don't believe they can find the perfect solution to a customer problem, but one way of looking at this is to ask yourself, 'Is it right for *now*?' When your service is just ahead of the curve in the areas in which it matters, and can evolve as needs and technologies change, then it's beautifully designed.

Service providers have always striven to compress the time lag between identifying a group of potential customers who want something new, and then giving it to them: the search for the 'new'. Of course, any examples we give here will be dated by the time you read this book because this is an area in which months, not years, are the yardstick. There's a metropolitan battle between food delivery outfits like UberEATS and Amazon Restaurants, which are encouraging us to eat in, and service businesses like OpenTable, which make it easy for us to eat out. So what makes these services 'right for now'? They serve our time-pressed lifestyles – which we've had for a while, of course – but they do it using technology, which makes it possible for them to offer a new speed and personalization of service. It feels spot-on for the moment.

So a beautifully designed service is connected to the moment in the best possible way, by being right for the marketplace, right for the time, right for the audience, and right for the prevailing culture of which it will soon become a part.

It's not just about appearance

Beautiful design isn't only about aesthetics. Of course, how your service is visually represented is important, but to connect emotionally with your customers it will need to weave together great looks, spot-on functionality, easy usability, top-level originality, and a timely sense of appropriateness for the occasion and the culture it's in. Restaurants, airports, shops and other service spaces in which the owners have invested in the design of the space, but not the people and their behaviours or the underlying service model, don't work well. Making all the elements of a service work elegantly together is how to appeal to those who use them.

The McDonald's restaurant chain has made some major changes to its design over recent years. When they decided to invest in their interiors to bring them in line with their new brand positioning, they could have implemented a simple visual face-lift. Instead, they were bolder. Not only did they do away with the much-loved plastic brashness of the previous yellow and red colours, moving to a more muted, natural palette, they also redesigned the food ordering system for their customers. By introducing self-service ordering points and a mobile app, they separated the ordering of the food from the collecting of it, reducing queuing times. This has obvious benefits for their customers and their business, as potential diners are now less likely to be put off by long queues at the counters. It was a genius move, because they responded to a key customer pain-point (the queues), while also recognizing that their customers today are more comfortable interacting with screens – in fact many prefer them.

It respects the details

It's the detail of design and delivery that determines a service's success. So much of what something is, is made up of what it does and how it works. You might have a great idea for a service, but until you've worked through layers of increasingly specific and detailed design, you can't be sure it's going to be good. An online service, for instance, could be conceptually brilliant but hard for people to use because the user experience isn't smooth enough, or the site isn't visually refined enough.

Earlier we mentioned taxi industry disruptor Uber. They knew they had to get sign-up and one-click booking and payment working seamlessly in their app. They were also aware that their customers needed to see an abundance of drivers in their area in order for them to feel confident in the service. Add to this the need to ensure a consistent level of vehicle quality and customer service from the drivers, and you get a feel for the level of detail involved.

It's designed for everyone

As you know, your customers aren't all the same. Some have particular difficulties because many services, including digital services, don't provision for people's particular disabilities. One in five people in the UK, for example, has some kind of impairment, which we've categorized into six main groups: mobility, dexterity, vision, hearing, cognitive, and social. The people in these groups represent a large chunk of spending power in the UK, which means if you only design your service for an able-bodied person, you'll be turning away revenue. Designing for everyone isn't just about being a responsible corporate citizen, it's about being commercial too.

In many countries the law requires providers to design and deliver services in ways that make them accessible for all. A beautifully designed service should work for everyone – it must be inclusive, accessible and usable by most people. Much is now known about the inclusive design of products, but less is discussed about services, so this is a field about which you can expect to see more debate in the future.

It just works

Designers are experts in crafting elegant solutions, which work well within the constraints of the physical world. A beautifully designed service comes from achieving the very best experience from the fewest moving parts, hiding the complexity of what's needed for it to operate from the customer and even from the staff delivering it. Great services are delightful because they're easy and enjoyable to both use and deliver.

Adam suggests that a beautifully designed service is one that '…works without thought. Effortless'. He compares the beauty you can strive for in service design to the beauty and elegance that mathematicians see in a brilliant mathematical proof. It's not necessarily a material beauty but it is a sense that the service as a system is 'fit for purpose'. It does a great job for the customer and it does so with ease; it just flows.

Four skills to help you tune in to beautiful service design

Now we know what a beautifully designed service looks like, but how do we create one? We can see it's not just about aesthetics. It's about how it looks and feels, how it works, whether it's distinctive and original, and right for the time and culture. Not only that, but all the moving parts should fit seamlessly together. Here are four skills you can develop to tune in to beautiful service design:

- understanding what services are made of and yours in particular;
- getting into the habit of spotting what good looks like and talking about it;
- not being afraid to imagine what you yourself would enjoy;
- being prepared to defend what makes it beautiful.

Understanding what services are made of

As we mentioned before, a beautifully designed service is made up of many moving parts, all of which should work smoothly together without the customer, or even the service staff, realizing. A business will also need to monitor it for effectiveness. So a service is made up of:

1 its parts;

2 how those parts are connected;

3 how they work together to deliver the service;

4 the metrics and performance thresholds used to measure them.

Fine-tune your ability to spot what good looks like

It's not easy being a professional, viewing the world as you do at work while at the same time experiencing it as a regular consumer. Yet viewing the world as a consumer is a useful professional skill to learn. If you're to discover new, amazing services, elements of which might work for your own business incredibly well, you need to train your mind to spot them.

Take the time to close your eyes and recall your own experiences and feelings about a service you've recently used (this may feel odd but it's worth doing). Step away from your assumptions and dig deep to understand what took place to engender this feeling. What is it you remember about the experience once your brain has had time to forget?

Don't be afraid to imagine what you yourself would enjoy

If you're like most people, there's something odd that happens to you as soon as you walk into the office: you forget that, like your customers, you're human too – you're all humans. The culture of your organization probably exacerbates this by over-emphasizing the significance of data as proof of the validity of potential new solutions, so your instinct becomes downgraded and opportunities are lost. Even collective common sense comes under suspicion when seemingly decisive numbers are on the meeting room screen. But as a human being you have a valid point to make about what other humans value and enjoy.

This may seem fairly obvious, but it's a subversive point to make. We all understand that it's terrible practice to design only for yourself, especially if you, or people like you, are not the target users of the service. And this is absolutely true – you should always work with good insights about the customers you're designing for. However (and here's the ambiguity), at some level we human beings value and enjoy the same things. The danger comes when you make assumptions about everyone based on your own preferences and feelings. You're probably right, but you should always test your assumptions. So design for humans, of which you are one, but not just for yourself.

Be prepared to defend the aspects of a solution that make it beautiful

In a world in which a business can, in theory, make anything and the temptation is to make everything, you should find a way to understand how to balance beauty with the objective of delivery. When budget holders are looking to reduce costs, and stakeholders are keen to see quick, easy results, it can be tempting to cut corners. And there's nothing wrong with placing some quick wins into your plan, of course (we'll cover that later in the book).

But have you identified the elements of your service that make it beautifully designed? Because those are the things that make it worth the time, money and effort you're expending. These are the aspects that will spark conversations between your customers and their friends. And these are the features that will keep them coming back for more.

Here are five questions to test the beauty and greatness of your service design:

- **Distinctiveness and originality:** does your solution bring something new and exciting to your customers' world?

- **Clear expression of your brand:** does your solution make sense coming from this brand, and does it enhance your brand perception?

- **Exceeding consumers' expectations:** is your solution an improvement not only on what you currently do, but on what else is out there shaping customers' expectations?

- **Clear value proposition:** do you have one, and is it marketable? Can you make it work, do it consistently over time, and build on it?

- **Workability for everyone:** does your solution work for your diverse customer groups with their broad range of needs and abilities?

Key takeaways

- A beautifully designed service gives you a competitive advantage because it looks fantastic, is easy to use and solves your customers' problems elegantly – all at the same time. It also costs less to operate than a poorly designed service.
- Beautiful service design is easier to recognize when you see it than to define in the abstract, but has the following qualities:
  - It connects emotionally with your customers, so they find it a pleasure to use and come back again and again.
  - It contains a striking element of originality, which draws people to it.
  - It's right for now, by being spot-on for the marketplace, your customers and the prevailing culture.
  - It takes into account usability as well as appearance – in other words, it's not just about looks but about giving your customers an operationally elegant experience.
  - It's been thought through in enough detail to get to the heart of what your customers want from it. It's more than a good idea; it works.
  - It 'just works' in a way that's easy and enjoyable for your customers to use, and for you to deliver.
  - It works for all your customer groups and takes into account their diverse needs and any particular difficulties they may have with using it.
- Designing your service beautifully isn't easy, but if you follow these principles you'll not go far wrong:
  - Understand the moving parts that make up your service so you can make them work together without friction.
  - Fine-tune your ability to spot what good looks like, by noticing when you experience a fabulous service yourself.
  - Be honest about your own human preference for beautiful services – would your company's offering delight you?
  - Be brave enough to argue the case internally for creating beautiful services your customers will love to use.

Develop a clear value case   09

Think back to the last time someone came to you with a bright idea at work. How did you react? You might have been excited by the potential, but you'd have wanted more information before you committed. How much effort and cost would be involved? What might be the impact on existing projects? Most importantly, what kind of results could you expect? On top of that you probably wanted the information up front, clearly and concisely. No-one feels motivated to make a decision about something when it's presented in a way that leaves the idea and its value unclear. In other words, what you needed was a clear case to be made and made in a way that excited you and gave you the assurances you needed to feel safe to proceed.

Large organizations often have well-practised processes, formulae and criteria for guiding and making decisions. Often these methods have been optimized over time with evidence from the outcomes of many previous decisions. However, which formulae or criteria should you apply when you're setting out to do something very new; to design a service and deliver an experience to your customers for which there is no data? The design toolkit can help here too. It requires an imaginative step. Working creatively and collaboratively on a design project to the point where you can prototype and then pilot a new solution quickly is, in our view, the best way to build the case that a new solution can succeed in the market.

Without historical data or a formula to rely on, a 'design project' gives you the structure and tools with which to demonstrate rigour by systematically involving a range of experts (including your frontline colleagues and your customers) and by building things quickly and testing that you can gather 'evidence from the future'. What these approaches allow you to do is tell a story about the holistic value of the investment you're proposing, beyond the conventional cost and benefit conversation (which remains important too).

Why is it so important to develop a well-structured and well-argued case to invest in what you've designed for your customers? Because there will be people in your organization who still see 'customer experience' only as a cost – something the business must do to reduce customer complaints. It can't be assumed that all your senior stakeholders will see the holistic value of the case you're making – you must bring the strategic case to life.

In this chapter, we'll look at the distinguishing features of a clear value case for new or redesigned services and experiences and what you can do to develop your own.

Why is developing a clear value case so important?

There are two main reasons for taking the time and effort to create a strong and compelling case for your vision:

- It reassures decision-makers.
- It means you can highlight the broadest benefits, not just the costs.

A clear case makes everyone feel comfortable with what you're proposing

Even if you've created a beautiful design and built consensus around it, and even if your vision is compelling and you can describe it in concrete terms, decision-makers in your business will want to have more certainty around your idea. One thing's for sure: your vision won't make it to market unless senior hearts and minds are happy with the direction.

In the beginning, the energy and intrigue you've created via your project, the insights you've gleaned from research, and the originality of your vision are enough to carry most people along. But quite rightly there will be some in your organization who, because of their character or role, feel the need for well-evidenced arguments to back this up. All decision-makers need to feel happy that the work they'll be doing to transform the service and the organization is for the right reasons. The good news is that once minds are won over, hearts are not usually far behind. In our experience, those who demand this rigour are not out to extinguish your vision – they just want to be certain it'll succeed. A clear case reassures decision-makers and, like the vision itself, serves as a reference point throughout to keep people motivated and on track.

It allows you to highlight the broadest benefits, not just the costs

A typical business case for a new project tends to focus on cost and revenue: if we spend this amount of money, we'll make this amount back. However, when your vision involves creating something totally new for your business (and, potentially, for your customers), the standard approaches to calculating benefits and return on investment may not readily apply. Of course, the commercial element is important, but what we also encourage our clients to do is to think about the benefits of new services and experiences in the broadest sense.

You need to be precise about the benefits your business needs to realize. Are you looking to make or save money by increasing customer loyalty, cementing your brand reputation, or developing your colleagues and frontline staff so that they sell more of your products and services or resolve customers' problems first time? Do you need to encourage more of your customers to 'self-serve' and in ways that don't annoy them? Do you need to improve your customer satisfaction scores to improve your reputation with your industry regulator or in advance of a business sale? Do you need to reposition your brand in the minds of your customers as your market changes? Do you need to implement a bold customer-driven idea to shift your internal culture?

The major challenge you have with assessing the total business benefit of your plan is its long-term nature; it may not materialize in full for several years, and this can be an obstacle if you're not careful. At that point, decision-makers may revert to assessing the costs alone and paring your proposals back to what will have impact immediately, which can result in your great ideas being compromised or even cancelled altogether.

By taking a design-led approach to developing your business case, you're focusing your teams on total value creation from the start. This means you're able to justify looking at the benefits in a holistic way, including the 'softer' aspects, such as your business being more attractive to external service partners.

What makes a case clear?

There are many elements to a clear case, and embedded within them are pointers as to how to create one. In summary they are:

- a strong imperative;
- quantifiable benefits;
- a strong investment case;
- the ability to show that there's already a level of consensus that your proposals are worthwhile.

Let's look at what makes a clear case.

A strong imperative

This seems kind of obvious, yet so many business cases or project initiation documents we see don't make it clear why a project is necessary or really get to the crux of the business need. When your project encapsulates a strong imperative for action, it will seem inconceivable to those around you not to do it. This needs to be understood by your whole business.

So what could these imperatives consist of? They might be a regulatory change, a shift in your customers' expectations (for instance, you've got behind with technology and your customers are starting to drift away), or a market development (new competitors have entered your space and you need to show you're better than them).

It's also good to look at this from the opposite point of view: what would be the cost of *not* developing and enacting your vision? Would you be in contravention of a new guideline or law? Would you see a slow but steady loss of customer loyalty and sales? Or would you be laying yourself open to being decimated by other operators in your sector? The cost of not taking action should be brought vividly to life. Now is no time for subtlety; as long as you can back up your argument with evidence and are able to get across your points clearly and persuasively, you are pretty much guaranteed to be listened to.

So a clear case is one in which there's a strong imperative to change. It's also one that builds in consensus and confidence through collaboration in the design process, and by grounding your vision with simple insights, data and reasoned arguments.

Benefits to both your customers and your business are quantifiable

We talked earlier about your clear case not being based on numbers alone but also on broader benefits, and that's still true. But, as with everything in business, figures do hold sway, which means you need to get your numbers lined up in such a way that they support your case. These figures may come from various sources, such as finance, consumer research and market insight.

Bear in mind that your organization might not necessarily currently collect the data you need. You want to build a case for a future scenario that your customers haven't yet experienced, so you're bound to lack some of the hard facts and figures you'd ideally like. What you might possess, though, are 'proxy measures'; indicators you can quantify about your business, customer base or marketplace that give a concrete indication that your case is sound. For example, if you're in the travel industry you might have seen a rise in the popularity of family holiday packages aimed at multigenerational families; even if you don't have internal data to back this up, you could collect together the evidence you need from external sources.

The investment case is strong

Your vision will take resources to implement, so your investment case must stack up. From our experience, it's likely you'll be asked for investment proposals with several different scales of investment. If you've been through a process of roadmapping the portfolio of changes you want to make, you'll be able to show how and when you can have the maximum impact on your customers with only an initial investment. A top mark for effort will come your way if you can propose a range of propositions and customer experiences at different levels of investment. However, if you do, be sure to be clear about the benefits that won't be realized with less investment, and how much longer it will take without the cash in place.

If you're going to state the benefits that your project and its delivery could realize, then it's important also to be clear on the timeframe and the dependencies associated with these benefits. Your business can't realize the benefits without making the changes and your senior stakeholders need to be clear on this. It's important to link the components of your value case to specifics about when certain capabilities will need to be in place and when certain customer propositions and experiences will need to have made it out there.

Johanna from Finnair uses customer data generated through airport operations and transactions to help build the case for change:

> *It's important to have a business case. Financial people need the numbers. And it's so much easier than it was ten years ago. In the past, it was much more difficult to prove the case for investment in the experience but now we have the*

data, we can show cause and effect more clearly. We can track behaviour and this is very important when you're looking at customer loyalty. Today we can tell a coherent story about why and how we want to improve the experience and the impact it will have.

It's worth looking at the operational data your business routinely captures and that your board values and exploring whether you can link the benefits you can attain for your customer to these operational metrics in some way.

It has agreement across the business

When there's consensus and confidence among your stakeholders, there's little that can get in the way of your project. But you'll only achieve this if they all understand why others see it as valuable; they need to feel that certainty from their colleagues as well as for themselves. Different people, of course, have different perspectives. It's good if your case shows you understand those viewpoints; even demonstrating that you appreciate them is often enough to allow a productive discussion to take place.

Of course, the best way to develop consensus is to involve people in the process of research, conceptualization and design of new solutions, so that different perspectives can be shared early and throughout and issues resolved along the way.

How to create a clear case

As you can see, developing a clear case for implementing your vision is critical to getting the support you need. Business decisions are never made purely on instinct – and rightly so – which means a solid and persuasive proposal is one of the first tools you'll need. So how do you go about building your case? There are a number of approaches to this, which all need to work together. What's more, they involve empathizing with decision-makers who aren't bought-in to your idea, so you'll need your creative imagination and intuition to play a strong role.

In summary, here's how to create a clear case:

- get clear on the benefits;
- show how you'll realize them;
- prove it in principle first;
- demonstrate there's excitement around the business;

- pilot with a group of customers and gather data;
- create a clear plan.

Identify the benefits in the broadest sense, not just the financial ones

You've established your vision, so now start with the strategic element of your case; in other words, how what you're proposing to do will contribute towards fulfilling that original purpose. Your case needs to inspire as well as justify, so focusing on financial return on investment alone is not enough. What's exciting about it? What will motivate people to support you? What will it give your customers, so they return to you again and again?

Trace your plan directly back to the benefits you've set out to realize

Whatever it is that your business needs, these benefits need to be clear and agreed and then it must be possible for you to trace each tangible element of your proposed service design back to these benefits in as direct a way as possible. Here's a simple illustration of how you could construct this 'value logic':

1 **Tangible things**: We're going to design and deploy these things...

2 **Changes in customers' behaviours**: This will mean our customers (and colleagues) can and will...

3 **Outcomes**: We'll know this is having a positive impact when we see...

4 **Benefits**: Over time this will drive these metrics...

5 **Strategic story**: Which will drive the business towards realizing this vision.

Prove your solution in principle first by prototyping

Managing risk is what many organizations base their decisions on, and it so happens that design thinking is well placed to help them do that. With their focus firmly on the customer, design-led methods enable you to see what's most important in your service, so you can hone in on the essentials and prove their validity before you go any further.

One of the best ways to do this is through prototyping your proposed service. This is an incredibly powerful way of getting buy-in from decision-makers, because it allows you to test future solutions today. It means everyone can 'see' the solution in a way they can't when it's just an idea on paper.

We worked with one UK mobile phone company that wanted to understand whether offering appointments in its retail stores would be helpful for its customers. We spent a week in its mocked-up store at their headquarters, experimenting with different scenarios by which the operator could orchestrate an appointment service. We invited store colleagues to take part, playing themselves and taking on the role of customers (they knew their customers better than anyone). Together we role-played different situations with different imagined customers and we mocked-up digital touchpoints using paper and card. Through this we could get a feel for whether or not the idea of offering appointments to customers in stores was workable, and what would need to change in the operation of stores and online. With the service designed in principle, we then set out the technical requirements for the booking platform, and defined the tasks that colleagues in-store and in the contact centre would need to perform.

Figure 9.1   Prototyping the service design of a premium, fast-track route through airport security in a hangar on the edge of the airport

This effort can go a long way towards making your case clear, because it 'proves' your proposals are sound in principle before you put them into practice. It also generates some data, which helps you quantify your case. You can build confidence and consensus through service prototyping, as key people can be exposed to the solution early and at little cost. This takes some of the heat out of major decisions down the line.

By the way, prototyping (the scenario we explained above) isn't the same as piloting. Prototyping starts much earlier, as it's exploratory. Piloting involves testing a live version of your service in a specific location or with a group of customers or colleagues; it's more risky and costly than prototyping, and happens much later in the to-market process. Failing early and learning through doing is becoming increasingly attractive to businesses, and you might find the idea of prototyping is accepted more readily than a full-blown pilot.

Show that your colleagues and customers are already excited by your idea

Social proof goes a long way towards convincing decision-makers that your case is worth considering. Once a critical mass of colleagues is enthused by the ideas and solutions emerging, this will encourage others to pay attention to your case. And if you can show, through research, prototyping or agile development, that your customers are also keen for you to make these changes, this will help to cement your position.

Pilot in full with a small group of customers and gather data to cement your case

With the grand ambition to be the world's best for service in their industry, the Hyundai Motor Company needed some real evidence of the effectiveness of any new retail experience and customer service model. So they decided to build and test it. And they didn't choose a small neighbourhood dealership but instead a high-profile site in Seoul's Dosan neighbourhood, known for luxury retail. Yeonhee Lee explains how delivering the pilot and getting the data were essential to the programme moving forward. As she puts it:

The 'Serve With Pride' customer service model we developed with Engine was a strong driver for the expansion of the Motorstudio brand experience. After we opened Hyundai Motorstudio on Dosan Street (an area in the downtown commercial area of Seoul synonymous with luxury automotive retail), we could reveal its performance. The confidence of internal stakeholders grew and we could move forward much faster. Since the first Motorstudio retail model store opened we've been using it as a laboratory to further develop the model. The desire to use the Dosan store as a laboratory came from our top management, which shows that we all share the same view and philosophy.

As an automotive manufacturer, it's not easy to gain investment in service, for either software or people. However, because we had a solid design process and good insights from customer research, we were able to develop a compelling vision and describe the impact that investment would have. We were able to put great investment into service, establishing the 'Serve With Pride' model for our retail staff and developing the new 'Guru' role, which is very different from how service has always been delivered in our retail stores.

With one of the largest airports in the world to transform, and plans for a new and even larger one, our client Dubai Airports had to convince teams of the value of aspiring to more and working differently before major programmes could progress. Frank describes the role of pilot projects in making the case:

As this whole thing was so new to the organization, we needed to prove our case. So, we set up several pilot projects that – we hoped – would demonstrate impact and realize benefits in key parts of the airport experience and would make it obvious that a different way of working was required; one that was design-led and multidisciplinary. We set up one pilot to design and deploy an enhanced frontline hospitality team and one to improve the provision of information for passengers. While we were developing concepts and designing solutions to pilot, we spotted benefits that new solutions could realize for passengers and the business; these became the metrics by which we'd evaluate the pilots.

Where there was already a mechanism for measurement in place we used it, and established an as-is baseline. But we realized that there was no mechanism for assessing the 'service style' of frontline hospitality colleagues; in other words, how they interacted with passengers. So, we designed an evaluation framework and baselined this too.

Once the pilots were running we were able to look at specific data points, using metrics that the business already understood, in order to make the case for the full roll-out of the service. Both pilots showed positive impact in most areas and were given the green light for full implementation. And, some aspects were dropped because they just didn't work.

Not only did the positive results demonstrate the impact on the passenger but they also reflected positively on the methodology we'd developed for training and measurement. Developing a hospitality team required the ongoing involvement of the Research and Development, Marketing and Branding, Commercial, Business Technology, Operations, Training, and Talent and Development teams to make it work. Through these projects we proved that new design-led ways of working were not only impactful but necessary.

Include a clear high-level plan and implementation approach

To secure the confidence of senior people your proposal must feel do-able. Show you've got an outline plan for implementation. As we mentioned above, anticipating the potential issues and risks in your project and in the implementation of your service will lend your plans credibility, and more so if you can show how you would tackle the problems. Think backwards from your end goal so you know what needs to happen at every stage of the journey, and plot it out in an attractive visual format so others can understand it. More on this in the next chapter.

Here are five questions to check the clarity of your case:

- **Evidence:** have you quantified the value of it to your customers and the business?

- **Able to be implemented:** are your stakeholders confident that your solution can be delivered?

- **Investment case:** does it stack up? Have you assessed your costs based on the total benefits to your business and brand?

- **Agreement:** does everyone agree with your case and can internal teams confidently present it, thereby influencing other stakeholders?

- **Strong imperative:** does your case create an unstoppable momentum to act among your senior stakeholders?

Key takeaways

- Your compelling vision needs an equally compelling case to be made for it if it's to survive the challenges it will face throughout your organization. This means you must tell a great story about it, and keep telling it in a way that excites and motivates people.

- A clear case means everyone can feel comfortable with your project – once minds are won over, hearts are never far behind.

- Highlighting the benefits, rather than just the costs, will be key to developing your case. Make these tangible so your colleagues can see what you plan to create, how it will change things for your customers, what the outcomes will be, and the benefits of these – all wrapped up in an easy-to-tell story.

- A clear case contains:
  - an undisputable reason why this change must happen;
  - quantifiable benefits both for your customers and your business, even if that means generating new research;
  - a reasoned case for the kind of investment levels you're asking for, so the figures stack up;
  - answers to the questions you'll be asked about how practical your plans are;
  - a realistic timeframe;
  - evidence of consensus and that key people have contributed to the vision.

- You can create a clear case by:
  - vividly presenting the world of your customer and new insights about them that are driving design and change;
  - being clear about the benefits of your service design, and not just in a financial sense;
  - joining the dots between the tangible features of your service design, the specific benefits it will realize and the vision you're all working towards;
  - establishing how you'll measure the impact of redesign;
  - prototyping and piloting your proposed service to prove its viability in full or in part – this also helps you to fail early and learn through doing;
  - showing others are already excited by your idea, as social proof.

Make it ready to 10 build

You're planning an extension to your house, with a spacious living area downstairs and a spare bedroom above. It's going to look fantastic. Eager to get started, you sketch out on a piece of paper how it will look. Next you label the different parts to show what goes where, so your builder will know what to do. It couldn't be clearer. What could possibly go wrong?

Plenty, of course. In reality, you wouldn't dream of expecting your builder to interpret your rough sketch accurately enough to ensure you get the home extension of your dreams. In the process of doing that, he's bound to make some assumptions that don't match your vision. He'll misinterpret the size of the windows, or he'll turn that scenic archway into a doorframe. Just as likely, he'll be tempted to cut corners on costs because you've not told him exactly how you want him to do the job and which elements really matter to you.

It's the same with the design of your new service. Much has to happen between the sign-off on your vision and its deployment within the real-world constraints of your business. This puts the value that you've 'designed-in' at risk of erosion. Many teams will be involved and many decisions will be made along the way, so your role as service designer at this point is to help translate the vision for your service and experience into a detailed design with a clear description of the capabilities necessary for making it a reality. Everybody will need to be clear about which specific features and qualities will make your solution a success.

Going back to the plans for your house extension, instead of handing your sketches over to the builder, a wiser move would be to hire an architect to draw up some proper plans. The drawings would be extremely detailed, specifying the materials and measurements to be used and how the construction should work. After all, this is a project in which you're investing a large amount of money and that, when finished, will give you a wonderful place to live.

What's the difference between the architect's drawings and your own? It's simple: they make your extension *ready to build*. Instead of leaving everything to your builder's own interpretation, they take away the guess-work so you end up with something that matches your initial vision as closely as possible, and won't fall down. In the same way, your plans for your new service and customer experience need to be drawn up as a blueprint, or a set of detailed descriptions of how your service will operate. This will contain enough definition and depth to guide your implementation teams to the right actions, and will show at least a partial solution to the practical problems you've identified while developing your clear case. It will also highlight the elements of your plans that are the most important – the ones you don't want to compromise on. The service blueprint is what turns your plans into a service design package, instead of a bunch of top-line ideas.

In this chapter we'll look at the important stage of preparing what's needed to ensure the solutions you've imagined for your customers are 'ready to build'. We'll look at why it's important to spend the time describing what's needed and exactly what will make the implementation of your solutions a success – and the risk of key details getting 'lost in translation'. We'll introduce the idea of a 'Design Package', a collection of documents that give you control over your design, help you communicate 'design intent', and serve as a reference for decision-making and measurement as you and your teams progress.

Why is creating a specification and plan that is ready to build so important?

There are four main reasons why you'll want to ensure your plans are specific and clear enough. A ready-to-build plan means:

- you'll avoid losing the subtle elements that you've shown will make your project and the resulting service a success;
- you won't come across nasty surprises further down the line;
- decision-makers are less likely to demand compromises;
- the moment when the design phase is completed is clear.

Much can get lost in translation once your design is signed off

In any service, it's often the subtleties that are a large part of making it a success; these can get lost once the realities of what's involved in the delivery become clear. This means your Design Package needs to contain enough detail to ensure your implementation teams can deliver it as it was intended, in a well-crafted and orchestrated way.

Ready-to-build blueprints also embed accountability into the process that follows. If your specification and plan make it clear, for instance, that the customer research you did six months ago showed that a particular element of your new service was critical, this removes the temptation to cut out this element when it starts proving difficult to implement. Instead, with the design rationale documented, everyone can understand what's going to make this project and the designed service a success, which means they'll need a strong counter-case if they disagree or choose not to implement it. The goal? Your customer experience transformation will get to market intact, without being heavily compromised by the people implementing it.

There are no nasty surprises when it comes to the technical and operational challenges of implementation

As we mentioned in the last chapter, making your design tangible as soon as possible through prototyping will reveal any potential technical and operational challenges early. This means the relevant work streams can explore alternative solutions before it's too late. The last thing you want is for operational gremlins to pop up during the implementation phase – they can cause delays and, potentially, be a deal breaker when it comes to your project going ahead.

It helps senior decision-makers clarify the implications of any compromises

Leaders in your organization should be able to evaluate the impact of any proposed changes to your design along the way, and to do this they need to understand how these will impact customers and the benefits you set out to realize.

Going back to our builder analogy, suppose your architect's drawing specifies a picture window, which looks out over a stunning view. This is a key factor in the success of your project, because it makes your extension special and unique. However, when the estimated costs arrive, this window turns out to be more costly than you'd thought. So now you have a decision to make. Do you press ahead with it despite that (maybe cutting corners elsewhere), or do you replace it with a normal window and lose the main element that makes the room desirable?

Without the detailed drawings and costing you wouldn't have known you had a problem. With them, you can see the full implications of whatever path you take. The result of this is that you're in control of what is and isn't compromised.

It marks an important shift of ownership for 'the design' from the project team to the teams that will implement it

The point at which a service design can be considered ready to build depends on the nature of the service, and how much of a departure it is from the services you currently deliver. One way to spot that moment is when the questions being asked by the implementation and delivery teams stop being about the clarity they are seeking from you or the business, and start being about the details of design and delivery. At this point, emotionally at least, they have started to own the project.

In most businesses, this is when the operational teams become committed to mobilization. Who is responsible for that step will vary by project. For instance, if you're building a new website, 'ready to build' isn't always a clear moment in time because you're likely to be designing and building simultaneously. However, if you're implementing a new service that involves many parts of your customer operation, there will be a more obvious moment when clearly articulated plans will be handed to delivery teams. Signing off the Design Package signals the moment when people and plans are ready to go.

How to make your Design Package ready to build

The Design Package is a collection of documentation and communications that describe the service and experience you've designed, and allow each of the teams in the next stages of the process to understand what they need to do. It's not a one-off item, and can evolve as your plans become more concrete.

Let's have a look at some of the things your service Design Package might specify:

- the vision with a narrative and case that links what you want to deliver for customers with their needs and the strategic drivers of your business;

- a description of the customers for your service and evidence of what they need and what they'll value about what you're proposing;

- a description of the various customer journeys your service will support;

- a description of what could go wrong for customers and an approach to eliminating or significantly reducing the likelihood of this;

- a description of how to turn your customers' negative experiences into positive ones;

- the identification and highlighting of your service's hallmark moments;

- a clarification of the capabilities you'll need;

- a plan for how you're going to deliver at each phase;

- a plan for making sure your external partners are involved at the right times;

- a plan for piloting your new service and experience;

- a plan to do full market testing;

- an approach to measurement.

The service and experience Design Package is a collection of documents (or 'design assets') that describe the designed solution before it's been implemented. This means that all others involved in making it happen know what needs to be built and, importantly, the features and quality of the design that most of all will ensure it realizes the intended benefits.

There are no fixed rules about what the Design Package should contain, as each project, service and organization is different. Services and experiences that are strongly digital in their focus and delivery will need technical documentation, use cases or user stories, and visualizations of key screens and flows to communicate key interactions or features of the service so that digital designers can understand the thinking that's been done to define what the digital products need to be able to do. On the other hand, a Design Package for a service and experience that will be delivered by people more than through digital channels will need to describe colleague roles and behaviours to inform recruitment, training and coaching. These Packages should describe the capabilities and policies that will enable frontline colleagues to act in the ways you want them to act. And you'll need to make it clear how customer operations teams will need to operate differently.

Design Packages for services and experiences that stitch together several channels may need all of this and, for example, specifications or at least requirements for physical spaces, customer communications, approaches to measurement and so on. We've listed and described below some of the most common and useful assets that we develop and use to help our clients make decisions and mobilize implementation and delivery teams as the phase of Conceptual Design transitions into Design and Build. There are many but we've picked these five because we use them the most:

1 Service Vision Wheel;

2 Concept of Experience;

3 To-be Customer Journey;

4 Service Blueprint;

5 Service Flatplan.

Service Vision Wheel

Redesigning a service and experience can feel like a large investment and commitment. It's therefore important that early on in your project you create a tangible, symbolic moment at which senior people can grasp and understand the big central idea that describes what you're aiming to create for your customers. And it's important that senior people sign off and sign up to the next steps. Most of our clients have something that defines their company's vision or operating principles and these statements have often been carefully considered and negotiated. However, it's important to understand what we're trying to achieve by instead depicting what we call a Service Vision Wheel.

At the end of the investigative and imaginative stages of new service development projects, we almost always end by drawing up such a wheel. Written in response to various inputs into the project, often including qualitative customer research, the wheel describes in words and images the essence or DNA of the service and experience we're setting out to create.

Figure 10.1 shows how these wheels are put together. From the centre outwards they contain:

- a central big idea that encapsulates the role you want your business to play in customers' lives or the main benefit you want your customers to enjoy (but you must be sure that they actually do want it);

- a set of statements that substantiate and help qualify this central idea, written as though to your customers, not as organizational objectives;

- a set of distinct offerings, features and experiences that will be the proof-points of the central idea. Some of these should be identified as 'hallmarks' and protected from compromise.

You can see all the different elements that need to be taken into account. When we help organizations create a branded service, we rebuild it from the bottom up, embedding a service proposition along the way. The proof-points and other elements that, although not distinctive, are necessary, will fill your Experience Portfolio (see Chapter 3) as you organize and manage their delivery.

Figure 10.1   The Vision Wheel describes the target service proposition for the business – a vision for the service that describes what needs to be built to make the vision a reality. It appears at an important stage in the process when key people in the business need to sign up to the direction of travel and remains as a reference for all subsequent design and delivery

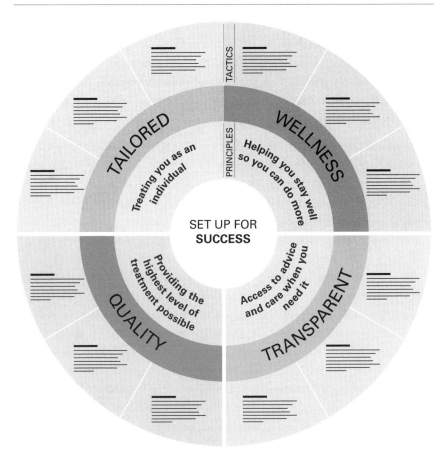

We asked Crispin from the Rail Delivery Group to reflect on the Vision Wheel we developed with him and his rail industry colleagues:

Our Vision Wheel conveys a huge amount of detail in a very clear, succinct and engaging way. I particularly like the wheel because it really helped me to get senior stakeholders on board in advance of the business case submission. The wheel has everything on one page, which really helps when you have two minutes to land the idea. The vision sits at the centre and is surrounded by a number of statements that describe the service we wanted to create. Surrounding these are the chosen customer propositions – the tangible elements of service delivery – that support the themes and deliver the vision. It's simple. It gives us a stand-alone product without explanation.

Vision Wheels contain around their central proposition a small number of customer experience principles that help to qualify the big idea and are used as a reference to inspire practical solutions and to sense-check decisions. The European energy company E.ON has defined and agreed a single set of service and experience design principles that are now used by all of E.ON's markets. When it comes to designing for their customers, the principles are routinely used to inspire thinking and sense-check plans and decisions. Keith Fletcher explains:

For us, our customer experience principles define what 'beautifully designed' means for the business and, importantly, for our customers. We've noticed that initiatives that ignore the principles tend not to feel right in the organization. This cultural shift is fascinating to observe and it's shaping much of our digital investment. Our brand personality of being simple, authentic, collaborative and creative is growing stronger every day; both service design and user experience design is at the heart of this.

Designing to our Customer Experience Principles has resulted in significantly stronger outcomes from a customer and organizational perspective. Our principle, 'We'll speak your language and make it simple', has led to us removing significant business complexity. For example, in Sweden, when it came around to a customer's contract renewal point we'd ask them to consider a raft of complex tariff choices – we've reduced this to just two simple ones. Simplifying the tariff structure then allowed us to live by another principle, 'We're the experts, so you don't have to be' – we've been able to clearly present renewable energy tariffs and to promote our investment in wind-powered generation.

Creating and signing off the Vision Wheel gives the project team and stakeholders confidence that the formative insights, strategic objectives and other drivers explored early on have been understood and reflected in a clear direction for the next stages of idea generation and experience design. If you do it well, your stakeholders will see the Vision Wheel as having successfully captured on paper what they feel should drive the development of the service. A great Vision Wheel is a great stepping-off point into the development of a *Concept of Experience* (see below).

Concept of Experience

What we call a 'Concept of Experience' is a visual depiction of the future end-to-end customer journey, which draws attention to key areas that have been identified as areas of focus because of the impact that improving them can have. It appears early and is necessarily conceptual but this document is important because senior people need to be kept close. You need them to be happy with these early areas of focus and to begin to get excited about how it could be. Helen from Dubai Airports told us about the impact having a Concept of Experience in place and signed off by the business had on their customer experience programme:

> *Communicating the vision for the experience, what we call the 'Concept of Experience', with other assets, including target customer journeys that clearly communicate what we want to build, meant we could all focus our efforts and move faster. With this work completed and the assets in place it felt like we moved faster in three months than we had in five years. For the first time, we had a very detailed vision for the customer experience that could be articulated to internal and business external partners. This made conversations about customer experience improvement and investment that had been difficult much easier.*
>
> *Internally, we knew the priorities and the route to implementation and we were able to improve the effectiveness and impact of work already in the plan.*
>
> *We were able to move quickly to the next level of detail, developing the 'Concept of Product' setting out how each product and service element would work and outlining the prerequisites and dependencies for the concepts to become a reality. This gave us a staged implementation plan effective across departments.*
>
> *Having this plan with the vision sat at the end of it meant we could coordinate across the business and with partners and agree a number of 'hero' projects that would give us some early results with customers. And we're already seeing positive results in NPS, operational and commercial metrics.*

Journey stages described in the Concept of Experience can include 'from' and 'to' statements, which describe the difference between the experience for customers today and how we want it to be for them. Data and insight from customer and colleague research is used to show why these areas are to be the focuses. On this high-level journey map we often include two drawn 'lines of emotion', the first tracing the emotional highs and lows for customers today and the second showing where we believe we can move the experience to with the concepts identified implemented.

The Concept of Experience appears at an early stage and is necessarily conceptual. It's part of the Design Package because it represents a set of decisions made early on about the important areas of focus for design or redesign. If you like, it's a visual executive summary of what is seen by the business as most important for the design of the experience. The Target Customer Journey (see below) provides greater, step-by-step detail.

Target (To-be) Customer Journey

We often need to show how the various new and improved features of a service, the operated channels and the products it contains, can be stitched together in a way that's most valuable to the customer and that works for the business. Even if you've figured out what the service you're designing will offer and what it will do, it's not until you must describe exactly how your customers will experience it that you begin to understand how it should work.

A Customer Journey Map is a tabulated representation of the end-to-end customer experience from the customer's point of view and shows how all the elements of the planned service come together as the customer experiences them. Specifically, a *Target (or To-be) Customer Journey Map* describes the experience your customers will have at each phase and stage of their journey with the service you're designing. And if you do a good job of creating one, the experience you're designing will start to become a lot more tangible for your colleagues to grasp. As a highly visual and practical document, it offers an alternative to dry requirements documents that fail to define the customer experience. With a Target Customer Journey, you'll be able to talk through what your customers will experience and highlight what's important. When you do you're sure to get a lot of valuable input but remember to focus the conversations on what your customers will value most first. Get this right, and the detail of implementation is developed later through 'blueprinting'.

Figure 10.2 The Concept of Experience is a high-level, one-page summary that allows stakeholders to quickly grasp and endorse or reframe the fundamental shifts needed for the experience. It is a useful framework to inform discussion and decisions on what matters most to customers and what areas the business should focus on

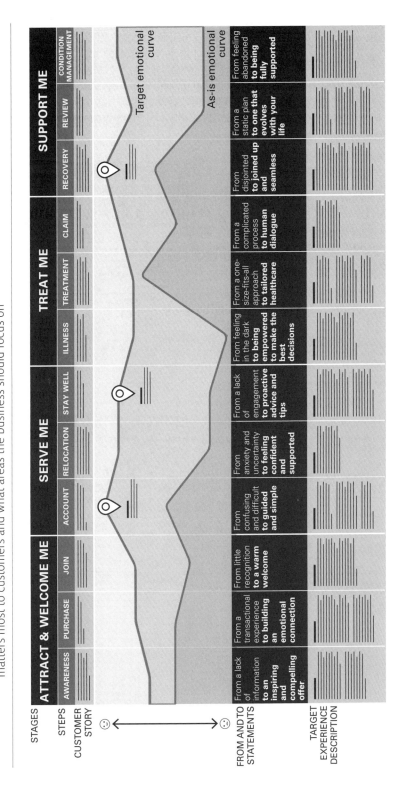

Figure 10.3 Target Customer Journey Maps are representations of a proposed end-to-end customer experience from the customer's point of view. They show how all the elements of the planned service come together as customers will experience them. There are many types of Customer Journey Map used by different business areas, from marketing and digital design to business process re-engineering. This example is an imagined section from a Target Customer Journey Map for the fictional Bermondsey Health Insurance International

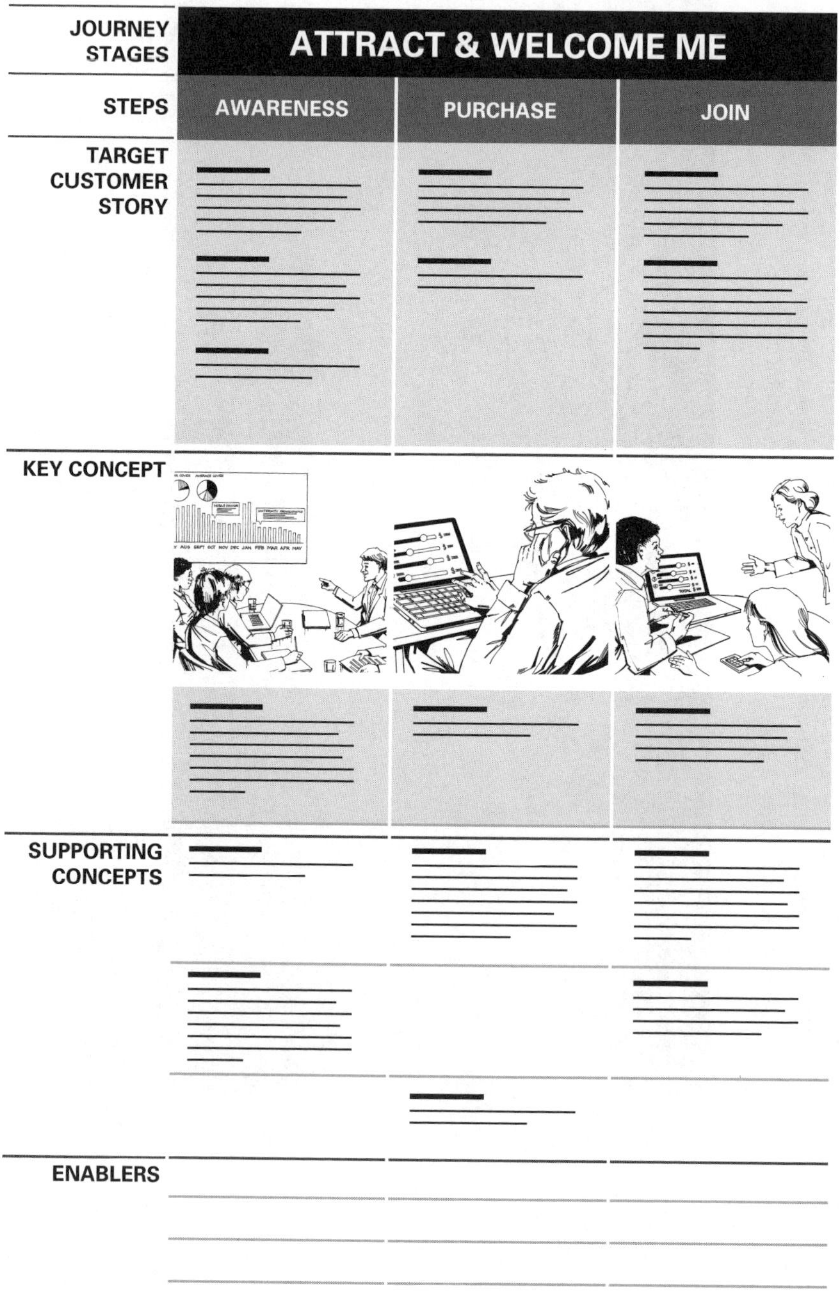

Service Blueprint

Consistency and coordination are essential in delivering a great proposition and experience, especially when many channels and teams need to work together. Without a single picture of what's required, there is a risk that each delivery area interprets the target design differently or delivers only the elements that are already on their roadmap. Translating what's been designed to give customers a great experience into new requirements for operational systems and teams is the role of the Service Blueprint.

The history of the Service Blueprint dates to the early 1980s (Shostack, 1984). It can be used as an analytical tool to understand the operation of a service today from the viewpoint of its customers or as a diagrammatical approach to communicating the target design. A Service Blueprint helps implementation and delivery teams understand what needs to be changed or built. Collaboratively, in cross-functional workshops, change requirements are developed based on the target experience, not the other way around.

A Service Blueprint extends the description of the Target Customer Journey (see above) to define exactly what's needed from people, processes, systems and data at each step of the 'To-be' Customer Journey. The Blueprint can also be used to identify what could and should be measured at points in the Customer Journey.

Crispin from the Rail Delivery Group describes how service blueprinting helped them to identify and keep track of the detail of what was required:

'The devil is always in the detail' and the devil always shows itself as the business embarks on change. The UK rail industry is a complex ecosystem and much of what's now in the plan, for example, for contact centres, will be delivered by operators who, although part of the same industry, are separate business units. The Service Blueprint helps the team to understand the detail and all the layers that underpin the proposition we'd designed together. The change plan not only helps to plan and execute change but also helps to reassure when faced with significant transformation. The Service Blueprint and change plan bring clarity and help us coordinate across our organizations.

Once created, the change requirements developed through blueprinting can be grouped and organized into a *Service Flatplan* (see below) and used to inform a Customer Experience Roadmap and delivery plans. As Samantha from Transport for London describes:

It's really important for us that outside of the large-scale investment cycles we can demonstrate a continual 'drip' of visible customer improvements, regardless of how small. We also know that to shift overall brand perception, customers need exposure to regular service improvement messages. The service 'blueprinting' process and 'roadmapping' the development of the customer experience as part of the service design programme identifies not only how you can make regular and incremental improvements to the customer experience, but helpfully where the sum of these changes provides you with a new and credible marketing message to engage customers with.

When it's doing its job your Service Blueprint will be accepted as a working document that represents what the business will look to build. You can hand it over to your Journey or Product Managers and implementation teams to own and add further detail. The Blueprint becomes the reference and management document for these roles as design transitions into planning and building.

Service Flatplan

Once journey design, blueprinting and other activities have been completed, there comes a realization that there is a lot to do – to change, build, buy or partner – in order to implement the vision for the service. A next step is to make sense of all of these requirements and begin to assess the capabilities you have in place already. Drawing up a Service Flatplan will help your team understand the service design that's being proposed by summarizing it on one page. It ensures that everybody is clear about what the main offers and touchpoints of the service will be and the enablers that exist or need to be developed in order to deliver what's been designed.

A Service Flatplan is a diagram made up of several boxes grouped and arranged in rows. Typically, the group at the top of the diagram summarizes the key offers and touchpoints with the service. The next rows summarize the main components of the operating platform; these are the enablers, which may be separated into macro and micro. Lastly, the Flatplan identifies the organizational capabilities required in order to develop and operate the platform and the services to customers.

Figure 10.4 An imagined section from a Service Blueprint for the fictional Bermondsey Health Insurance International. The Target Customer Journey is summarized at the top and written as 'experience requirements'. The change and build requirements needed to deliver the target experience are identified in the rows below

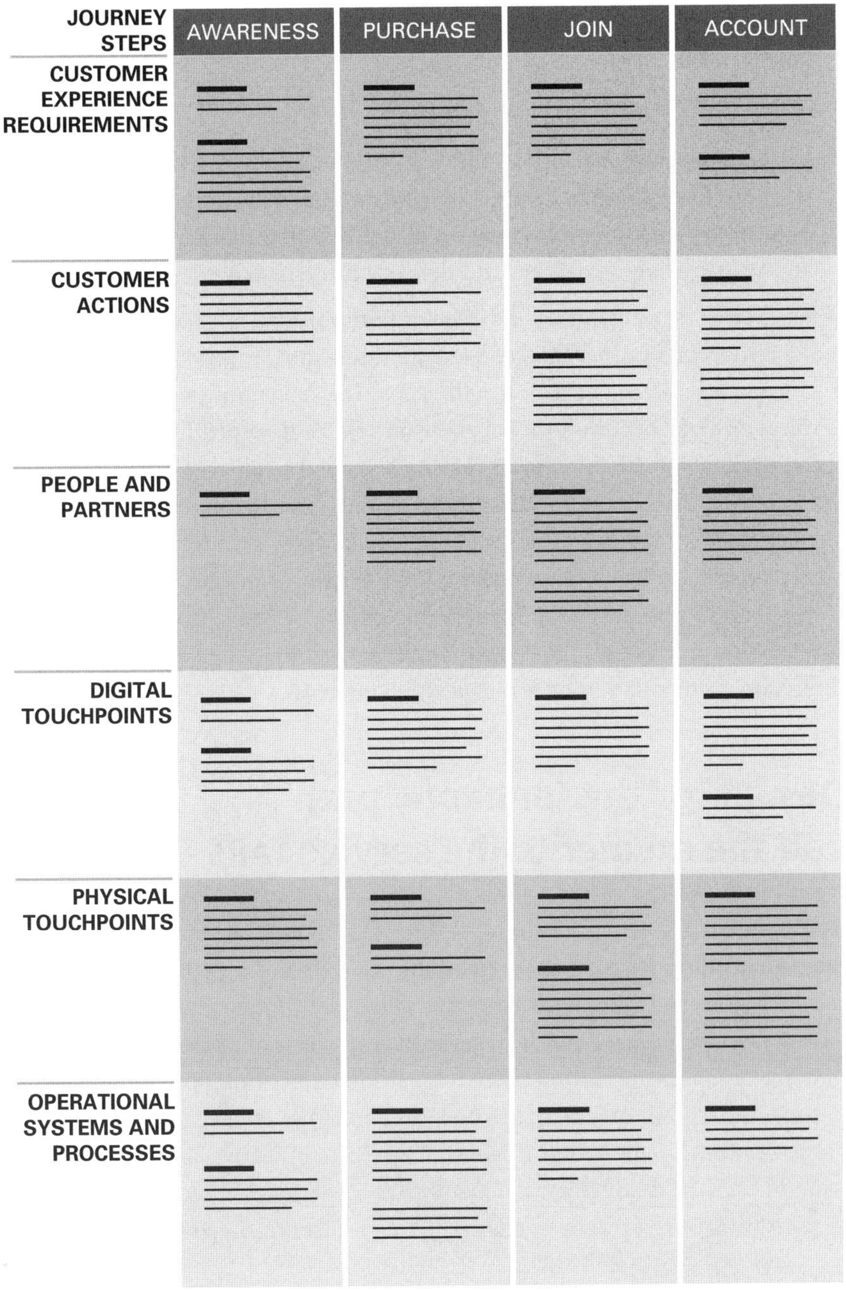

As a guide:

1 Capabilities refer to the strategic abilities an organization needs to consciously develop and mature over time in order to create and deliver value in a way that helps them realize their vision. Each ability will be drawn from a combination of products and services, processes, systems, data, people (knowledge, skills, behaviour and customer culture) and partnerships.

So, capabilities are built from a number of distinct enablers.

2 Enablers are tangible things that can be built, which make other things possible. For example, they may include digital solutions that may enable a number of features of a service, along with databases, frontline teams and roles, delivery partners and delivery infrastructure.

When you're setting out a Flatplan it's important to group change and build requirements (perhaps those generated during service blueprinting) into groups your organization will recognize. Your aim is to connect the features and offers within the service that you've designed for your customers with all the enablers and capabilities needed to deliver them. Drawing up a Service Flatplan will help you to understand the extent of what you have in place already and the gaps. They make the vision for the service and target experience feel like something your organization can actually build.

Here are a few more things to think about, design and include as part of your descriptive Design Package to ensure your design is complete and there's no ambiguity about what needs to be done.

Design for the 'unhappy path' and the moments the service fails

Remember that even if you're investing in new operational technologies, rebuilding your website and retraining your frontline colleagues, things will still go wrong for your customers. It's the moments when things go wrong (service failure) and how your business responds (service recovery) that are of increasing importance to customer retention, loyalty and reputation. Regardless of whether your customer made the mistake or your processes or systems failed in some way, your objective is to resolve this issue quickly and, ideally, turn a negative experience into a positive one. Service failure offers an opportunity for a great service recovery experience.

Figure 10.5 Anatomy of a Service Flatplan (example for the fictional Bermondsey Health Insurance International)

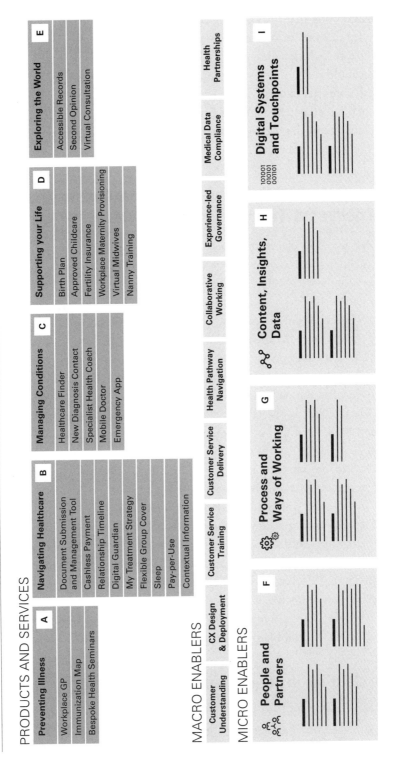

PRODUCTS AND SERVICES

Preventing Illness	A	Navigating Healthcare	B	Managing Conditions	C	Supporting your Life	D	Exploring the World	E
Workplace GP		Document Submission and Management Tool		Healthcare Finder		Birth Plan		Accessible Records	
Immunization Map		Cashless Payment		New Diagnosis Contact		Approved Childcare		Second Opinion	
Bespoke Health Seminars		Relationship Timeline		Specialist Health Coach		Fertility Insurance		Virtual Consultation	
		Digital Guardian		Mobile Doctor		Workplace Maternity Provisioning			
		My Treatment Strategy		Emergency App		Virtual Midwives			
		Flexible Group Cover				Nanny Training			
		Sleep							
		Pay-per-Use							
		Contextual Information							

MACRO ENABLERS

Customer Understanding	CX Design & Deployment	Customer Service Training	Customer Service Delivery	Health Pathway Navigation	Collaborative Working	Experience-led Governance	Medical Data Compliance	Health Partnerships

MICRO ENABLERS

F People and Partners

G Process and Ways of Working

H Content, Insights, Data

I Digital Systems and Touchpoints

So, accepting that if something can go wrong, it will go wrong, you can use the framework of a Customer Journey Map to identify points of service failure at each step and in each channel. Once you've imagined all the things that could go wrong, you'll be able to do two things. Firstly, assess how these potential failures can be eliminated or reduced significantly in number by making changes to the processes you operate. And secondly, imagine and design a great 'service recovery' experience for your customers in each case of failure along the journey.

Be sure to highlight the hallmark moments that must be delivered well

There are some elements of your customer experience that you may choose to make 'hallmark moments' – in other words, those points in customers' interactions with your business that give you the opportunity to amplify the values and personality of your brand and really prove the proposition that you've set out in your marketing. These are aspects of your service and experience that you know are both important to your customers and important for engendering the right perception of your brand in your customers' minds. These are the moments in which you can really signal the differences between you and your competitors.

Metro Bank in the UK can sign you up to a checking account and give you a bank card within 15 minutes of walking into one of their branches. NatWest Bank was the first UK bank to give its customers the ability to get cash from an ATM even if they had lost their bank card. Disney made queuing part of the entertainment. Amazon pioneered one-click shopping on the internet and Virgin Atlantic Airways (used to) service ice-cream to passengers during a movie. These hallmark moments may be in the details of behaviours and interactions or – like the ice-cream – explicit parts of your offer, but each allows you to own something (for a while at least). In your Design Package you'll clearly define these moments so they're given special attention when it comes to investing in making them work smoothly. In order for this to happen, you'll need to know why you chose them and exactly what should happen for them to give your service a buzz.

Be clear about the capabilities you need

These are the vital resources you'll require to implement the service and experience you've designed, so it's important they're thoroughly scoped. If there's anything you need to have in place, but currently don't (or not well enough), then you should address that as part of your plan. For instance, your CRM or billing systems might need updating to allow you to record further information about your customers or to present information to them in different ways, or you might have to buy in technical skills to integrate back-office systems into your customer website, or you might need to rethink your approach to recruiting frontline staff and invest in the skills of the team that delivers training.

When you ask yourself if you have the right delivery capabilities, there are four possible answers:

- We have them.

- We can build them ourselves.

- We can buy them in.

- We can partner with someone else to plug the gap.

It's easy for people across your business to get excited by your vision, but not so easy for them to think about what the business needs to have in order to achieve it. Your job is to work out if you've got the capabilities to deliver your plan, and be specific about what's required, otherwise it won't be ready to build.

Plan your programme to deliver marketable customer propositions at each phase

You're probably already used to creating programme plans, and product and customer experience roadmaps. If you were to launch a new app, for instance, you'd initially create a minimum viable product. The first launch (with limited functionality) would be Release One, in Release Two you'd add further elements, and in Release Three more still. This is your product roadmap. But the new service you're delivering may well be more complex than an app. It's not just one piece of software you're developing, it's a range of interlocking products, services and teams, which together make up a change portfolio.

We always look to organize this portfolio from the outside in, considering how to sequence the changes in a way that makes sense to customers. We don't want them to feel they're experiencing an ad hoc series of improvements, but rather a coordinated and meaningful sequence of new things for customers to do and experience. In this sense, the portfolio roadmap is more like a marketing campaign plan than a programme delivery plan. The trick is to line up the delivery of new products, services and capabilities into 'campaignable' launches. When you can achieve this, you'll see two benefits: your customers will experience value in each phase, and your business can shout about each phase completion in its marketing.

Let's look at an example from a major retailer we worked with. In response to changes in their marketplace, they developed a strategy to reposition their brand as being known for both excellent service and clever ways of using technology to personalize the shopping experience. This wasn't, they concluded, how consumers already saw them. We worked with them to design their service proposition, their services, and the experience for their customers, as they would be five years from now. This of course represented massive change, not only to their digital assets but also to how store staff sold to customers, how they designed their stores, and even to the products they sold. Rather than turn this problem over to their Corporate Programme Management Office, we ran workshops with their product managers and delivery experts. This resulted in a grouping of elements of the service or services into five campaignable phases; in fact, each of these could be described as customer propositions in their own right, with their own customer benefits.

Phase One prioritized the delivery of elements that made the retailer exciting again in consumers' eyes. The second phase was about encouraging customers to be more experimental, and to see the retailer as being able to give them new ideas. The third phase centred on ensuring customers saw the staff in the stores as enthusiastic experts. Although making all this happen was key, the business rightly decided it would take time to achieve. Improvements were made early on, but it wasn't until Phase Three that enough would be in place for the brand to start talking about their store staff again with confidence in their marketing.

Phase Four was about connecting their customers with the brand through better use of social tools and new approaches to content. This again would need time to build, which is why it was given its own phase. And Phase Five saw the launch of a new customer account proposition, making it more rewarding for their customers to have an account with the retailer. This was left until the end, as it took the retailer some time to develop their IT and logistics to the point at which a proposition centred around personalization could offer something of genuine value to their customers.

If you're like many managers we work with, you're proficient at creating roadmaps for individual projects, but find it harder to look at the programme as a whole. You'll talk to your digital team about developing the website, and to the learning and development team about staff training, but it's unlikely you're linking all those activities to a single view of what you want for your customers over the next few years. So, unlike a programme plan, which simply specifies who should be doing what and by when, your Customer Experience Portfolio and Roadmap are proposition-led and define the experience and capabilities you'll need to develop and by when.

Make sure your external partners are up to speed

Organizations often experience a dilemma about when to involve external suppliers in their service design project, especially if the project may kick-start a process of retendering. Of course, as part of developing your compelling vision and creating a clear case, you'll already have involved both internal and external partners, but *when* should you bring them on board?

Our advice is usually to invite your suppliers into your journey as soon as is practical, because you don't want to get to a point where you realize your contract or service level agreement excludes you from doing what you want. But you can involve them in ways that don't expose plans that they might feel threatened by or that may give them an advantage in any future tendering process. If you deliver your frontline customer support services through a third-party contractor, for instance, you won't want to discover that they aren't willing to support you in delivering your vision because their margins don't cater for the extra work, or because it conflicts with their other client commitments. Your relationship with your contractors can be pivotal to the quality of your proposed customer experience. The worst-case scenario is they may pay lip service to your vision and carry on as before, and the best is they're a fundamental part of transforming things for the better. How you negotiate with and manage them is therefore crucial.

Discuss with your team the challenges you might face and agree how you'll respond

With significant change comes significant adjustment, so you and everyone involved in the project need to be clear on how you're going to work. You can do this by asking each other a series of questions about:

- how you're going to work differently together both during and after the build phase;
- how your project will be overseen and decisions made;
- how you'll track progress;
- how you'll involve others;

- how you'll keep the right people engaged;
- how you'll remove barriers if they appear;
- where the money will come from;
- whether you have the right people and skills available and what external help is needed;
- how you'll decide when to engage your suppliers.

These questions and their discussion are important when it comes to undertaking any piece of work in your organization, but they are even more important when you're looking to make a more significant change to your services and business and when you're asking colleagues to think and work in a very different way.

Here are five questions to check whether your design is ready to build:

- **Designed to be built:** do you understand enough about what you need, both from your technology and from each delivery area, to make your project a success?
- **Pressure tested:** have you identified all the implementation and deployment issues early enough, through prototyping your service?
- **Enough detail:** have you defined your design in enough detail to ensure the implementation teams can deliver what you intended?
- **Well planned:** have you gained agreement that your development plan is complete and has the right level of information?
- **Ongoing oversight:** do you have the governance in place to limit the amount of compromises that get made on the design during the build?

Key takeaways

- Making your service design 'ready to build' avoids important elements of your plan being eroded as they pass through the hands of multiple teams and decision-makers. You need to make sure these details aren't lost because:
  - they're the parts that will make your service a success, so your plan needs to show why they're important;
  - you get your service to market more quickly when you don't encounter unexpected problems along the way;

- the implications of any future compromises will be clear when people can see the relevance of all the details;

- you'll avoid other people piggy-backing onto your programme and thereby losing focus and pace;

- operational teams need a proper plan in order to take ownership of the implementation of your vision – it's an important milestone for them.

- The Design Package is the collection of documents that describe the service and experience you've designed, and can evolve over time. It can include a Vision Wheel, a Concept of Experience, a Target Customer Journey, a Service Blueprint and a Service Flatplan.

- You can make your service design ready to build by:

- showing how different customer groups will use your service differently;

- anticipating the moments when the service will fail, and including solutions in the plan in advance;

- highlighting the hallmark moments in your customer experience that must always be delivered well – these are the elements that will give it the distinctiveness that's quintessentially yours;

- being up front about the resources you'll need to implement your vision;

- plotting your delivery programme so it resembles a marketing plan as much as a project plan;

- bringing your external partners into your process as soon as possible;

- opening a dialogue internally about how you're going to overcome any challenges you face, and how you're going to keep on track.

Reference

Shostack, G L (1984) Designing services that deliver, *Harvard Business Review*, **62** (1), pp 133–39

Create the right conditions 11

In some ways, getting a new or improved service to market is like cultivating a garden. As head gardener you've got your vision of how you want it to look, which enables you to decide what to plant and when. But you also need the right conditions for it to flourish. If the soil is too acidic, the sun too hot or the timing wrong, it will wither and die. On the other hand, if the conditions are favourable, it will thrive in a glorious display of colour and vegetation. Think of the people working on your project as being like those plants; they need the right environment for them to succeed, and it's up to you to provide it for as long as it takes.

Preparation is everything. With a complex project or portfolio of projects ahead of you, it's important that you and everyone involved knows what it's going to feel like to go through it, not just in terms of the steps you'll be taking but the challenges ahead for people's imaginations, risk profiles and mental energy. In the last chapter, we talked about how different managing a service transformation project is from other projects you may have worked on. This means your colleagues need to know why they're working in a new way.

In addition, it's human nature for initial enthusiasm to die away after a while; even your most motivated colleagues will need help. Service transformation programmes usually take many months and in some cases even years to deliver in full, and people can start to forget why they're doing them. After all, creating your vision happened quite a while ago; with countless developments being proposed and developed in the meantime, time passes and people forget what was agreed at the beginning. 'Can't we do this smaller, simpler project instead?' they may ask. It's your task to remind and *re-remind* them about the initial vision – the garden you're trying to grow.

You've no doubt experienced energetic launches for other projects in the past, with a motivating workshop setting everyone off on the right track. This is useful, but it's easy to assume holding the workshop somehow gets the job done. This is never the case. Your role is to plan the project stages so each subsequent workshop gives a point of review, and input into the next stage. The participants must feel as energized and productive as they did in the very first one. And, because this process might be a little different from how people are used to doing things, you'll need to prepare people for each stage.

So how do you create the right conditions for your project? Much of what you'll learn in this chapter will be relevant to any project you manage, not just to customer experience transformation. And you'll no doubt have your own knowledge, experience and skills to add. But we want to address this aspect of project management here because it's critical to getting the right services to market faster, particularly when the implications are transformative.

In this chapter we'll explain why setting and maintaining the right conditions is so important when you're running creative and collaborative projects that impact many parts of your business and aim to make significant changes. We'll describe how doing so helps you to maintain pace and avoid circling back. We'll discuss the importance of making change tangible quickly and maintaining momentum and people's interest and commitment, while still being focused on the vision.

Why is creating the right conditions so important?

When you invest in people's understanding, comfort and confidence with your project's direction, this both accelerates time to market and reduces the risk of failure. Remember, you're asking people to adopt new ways of working; service design involves looking at your services in a different way, and your project may be more challenging than many are used to. So why is it so important to create and sustain the right conditions for your project to flourish and your solutions to succeed through implementation?

Here are three good reasons:

- 'blockers' will be swiftly removed because everyone is signed up to the objective;
- the work will gather its own momentum;
- you won't waste time continually restating the purpose or the plan.

Let's expand briefly on each of these.

'Blockers' will be swiftly removed because everyone is signed up to the objective

There are various types of blockers that can bar your way as you progress your project. They can be people-based (such as political or personality-driven issues), budget-based, implementation-based (practical problems arising during the delivery) or market-based (when research and testing shows customers or partners feel differently about your service than you'd anticipated).

A key element of creating the right conditions is identifying and dealing with these impediments as quickly as possible. Don't be disheartened, because this is where your groundwork pays off. Blockers are more than likely caused by people who, for whatever reason, have chosen to prioritize something else. These people will need persuading and each may need a different approach. Some things to try:

- Use the evidence you prepared for your *value case*, and refocus discussions on the reasons why the business initiated the project.

- Restate the logical steps that demonstrate how implementing what's been designed will help the business to realize specific benefits.

- Remind people that realizing these benefits depends on delivering enough of the service and experience designed to shift customers' behaviour and change their perceptions of your business. If the key elements of the design aren't delivered then customers won't behave differently and the desired outcomes won't materialize.

- Show how new features of the service and specific customer experiences have been roadmapped and why implementation has been organized in this way, including the dependencies.

- Remind people of the prototyping and testing you carried out and the colleagues and other experts you involved in the design process.

- Show the impact of the small changes you've already been able to make.

The work will gather its own momentum

This is hard to quantify, but shows itself as a mood within your organization. You might start finding it easier to encourage teams to reach milestones, or get requests from new people to be involved. You'll also be receiving positive feedback from customers and suppliers. This feeling of, 'Yes! It's working', is a fundamental element of having the right conditions for success, because if its opposite is present you'll probably find the project is pulled or reduced in scope fairly quickly. Clare from PegasusLife describes the importance of creating urgency and keeping up the momentum:

> *Momentum is key – and you will only keep momentum if what you're doing is linked to your business objectives – otherwise your board becomes... bored. Some of our challenges became clear once we recognized that the whole business has a part to play in delivering the customer journey, for example, delivering our vision for the 'buying experience' means that we have to work as one and learn to move much more quickly. The property needs to be built on time. This is a customer group that doesn't always see itself as having time. So galvanizing a sense of ownership of the customer experience strategy across the organization has been key. Looking back, our vision should have encompassed the whole organization.*

While you're monitoring feedback, though, it's worth remembering the design process tends to 'dip' in the middle. This is when you, and others, may start to doubt you're doing the right thing. You'll need to reassure people to get through this phase, reminding them that this is a natural part of the project and it's worth persevering. It will help if you refer back to the clear case you made at the beginning, and keep measuring your progress against the baseline you set at that point. When you're able to imagine the end outcome and paint a picture of it to others, you'll keep everyone enthused.

You won't waste time continually restating the purpose or the plan

If you've done a great job of setting out and evidencing your vision, the case is clear and the design is both beautiful and well detailed, you'll have done much of the hard work needed to create the conditions for success. With this work done and your Design Package in place, you won't have to spend time reminding people why you're all doing what you're doing and you won't need to justify the design or the decisions that have been made. This saves time and energy and allows people to focus their efforts.

How to set and sustain the right conditions

You can see how powerful creating the right conditions for your customer experience transformation is. These conditions aren't always physical, but are more often emotional and mental. They comprise:

1 gathering a core team to help motivate you and others;

2 ensuring everyone has enough time and resources to do the job;

3 preparing for collaboration;

4 giving people reasons to believe in the cause;

5 keeping the conversation going with your customers;

6 making changes to the way you work;

7 being open to experimentation;

8 sticking with it.

Create a core group of willing and motivated people

This is essential. These are the people who'll be clear about why you're doing this project and how the design process is going to look and, more importantly, feel. They'll also be the ones to give you the support you need to keep going through the months ahead.

We like Harvard Leadership Professor John P Kotter's article in the *Harvard Business Review*, which explains the importance of creating a 'guiding coalition' when you're making significant change happen in your organization (Kotter, 2007). This coalition, he believes, doesn't necessarily need to include the most senior leaders in the company, but must be made up of enough people to create momentum for that transformation. How many does that mean? It depends on the size and scope of your project and your business, but Kotter's view is that a group of five, growing to 20 or even 50 in sizeable organizations, would be about right. This coalition needs to be engaged in the vision, motivated to make the required effort and willing to influence their networks.

Sean from Bupa is clear that if you don't have a committed and senior team at the centre of your project, you're unlikely to succeed. As he puts it:

> *The walls of marketing departments (and agencies!) are littered with great ideas and designs that no-one had any intention ever to implement. Only design a new target experience if the organization is fully committed to implement. You must have permission to play, which means the senior stakeholder must be the operational manager who owns the process.*

You need your guiding coalition because, by definition, the service you're setting out to create doesn't yet exist. This means the process can lack certainty for some people, especially at the start. Because of this, you'll want your core group to be made up of two broad personality types: realists and idealists. The idealists will be on your side from the beginning because what you're doing is exciting and different. They're the ones who'll feel most comfortable with the uncertainty, or will at least be happy to sustain their discomfort so as to make progress. The realists are equally important, though. They're the ones who'll stop your project becoming a flight of fancy by adding their pragmatism to the mix, and help you see things through to the end. To the realists you'll need to do a lot of explaining about the nature of the process and what you're going to need from them; they need to understand the value of what they'll achieve along the way. In addition to this core group, it's essential to have at least one very senior person to make your case and validate your project. This will give you that social proof.

(Kotter reprised and updated this idea in a book entitled *Accelerate*, in which he describes the idea of a 'strategy network' (Kotter, 2014), a group of people not confined to one team or department but distributed across the organization, with the skills and tools to instigate and propagate innovative practices. Such networks are slowly appearing in organizations we've worked with, such as E.ON Energy; however, many organizations still struggle to build guiding coalitions (not steering groups) or indeed strategy networks and they remain constrained by departmental structures and employ too few people with the right mindset.)

Make sure your core group has the physical and mental resources for your project

It's not unusual for us to have a highly enthusiastic kick-off meeting with a client's project team, only to never see half of them again because they've got other priorities within the business. It sounds obvious, but it's important to make sure your core team members have enough time to focus on your programme. This is because in addition to organizing and implementing the work, they'll also be learning through doing, investigating different options, influencing and reassuring their own teams, and gathering the information they need. There's a huge amount of time and effort involved. People may make warm noises about commitment but this probably needs to be negotiated one or two pay grades higher than them.

In addition to time constraints, you may find it's difficult for some people to get their heads around the new approaches and ideas you're asking them to engage with. For instance, what's the difference between a 'customer process' and a 'customer journey', or between customer 'segmentation' and customer 'persona'? Many of these concepts are highly interpretable (including the word 'concept') and everyone has a different view of what's needed. You'll need to be crystal clear about what your desired outputs are at every stage, and listen carefully to the views of others. It's easy to assume they understand and agree when they may not.

Another mental resource it's worth paying attention to is your commitment to keeping the flame of your initial vision alive in people's minds. We found that one of our long-term clients recently started drifting into implementing ad hoc mini projects, which weren't contributing to the overall service transformation they needed to reach. This is so easy to do. Once they reminded themselves about the more valuable goal to which they were committed, they got back on track.

'Co-creation is king' so prepare for collaboration

Services are interwoven systems of people, technology, information and commercial models that produce things of value to businesses and their customers. Because they are systems, designing and transforming services is as much a social activity as it is a technical or creative one. Creating the right conditions requires that the mechanisms for collaboration and communication are in place and working well. In the microcosm of an airport, the actors in the system and their dependence on each other are clearly visible, and even more so when things go wrong. Designing and transforming the services and experiences at an airport demands the means of collaboration. As Johanna from the airline Finnair describes:

> *In an airport environment, there are so many players: airlines, security agencies, retailers and so on. The challenge for the airport experience is to make all of these parts work together so for passengers it feels well orchestrated. For this reason, it was so important that we ran a very collaborative service design project – that we worked together as an airline and an airport to form a shared vision.*
>
> *Our service design projects help us to understand each other's perspectives and to align our views as we move forward. The project was marvellous because it fulfilled the strategic role of aligning our organizations. All around the world the airport process is largely the same – but today we're able to talk about the customer experience in a way that raises the bar.*

As part of the project we ran with Finnair and the airport operator Finavia, we were able to provide the mechanism and the platform for two organizations to form a much closer working relationship, which has helped ensure the success of their joint venture, the redevelopment of Helsinki Airport. Johanna gives as much credit to the design of the collaboration as to the design of the passenger experience:

We found the common will to openly and confidently talk about what was needed. We became a family. We were able to forget about aggressively pushing our own viewpoints and instead openly understand a 360-degree view of what our businesses and our customers needed. Of course, we are two businesses and there may be conflicting commercial objectives but we focused on common objectives to reach a common vision. After all, our end customers are the same. It's certainly true that there is something very open and straightforward about the Nordic culture and this builds trust. We don't have hidden agendas and this is a factor in sustaining the right conditions for collaboration towards a shared vision and roadmap for our organizations.

Sean describes how involving people from across your organization in the design of new services and experiences for your customers isn't just a nice thing to do. He suggests that doing so builds resilience into your project or programme:

Co-creation is king. By taking your people and customers on the creative journey with you, you'll create unstoppable momentum. Almost 200 employees and customers were involved in creating our target experience. By involving these people in the design process you create a type of moral authority that can push through barriers to implementation, and the process itself creates an expectation within the business that long-standing customer frustrations will finally be addressed.

As Stella Sangok Lee, our client from the Hyundai Motor Company told us, building the resilience needed to keep going requires that more than just the core project team have ownership of the vision and feel able and supported by the organization to take the design forward and deliver it:

It was clear that to be successful the project would need to create a compelling vision and a well-designed service model. However, when it came to implementation the project team faced various difficulties. We worked hard to empower our internal customers, particularly our colleagues in the retail stores, giving them the confidence to go further.

Give people reasons to believe in the cause

I'm sure all your colleagues mean well and want the business to succeed. They may also believe that serving your customers well serves the business well. Yet it's a mistake to assume that everybody around you sees a problem or sees the need for a new solution. To create the right conditions for success you'll need to understand who believes in the cause and who needs convincing. Sceptics can be useful within the design process if they are prepared to be constructive, because they challenge assumptions and say it like it is. They provide a valuable dose of pragmatism. But too many sceptical voices, feeding off each other's recalcitrant attitude towards the process or the goal, can derail progress and erode the ability of others to remain positive.

Interestingly, sceptics do often believe in the cause, but they either lack the imaginative step needed to see there are problems or ways to improve, or they don't believe in the ability of the organization to deliver. Here's where a well-evidenced problem statement, a compelling vision, a clear benefits case and a realistic plan can turn sceptics into allies and advocates. Clare from PegasusLife describes the work she put in to convince sales and service teams that improving the experience for prospects of selling their assisted living properties and services would drive sales. Clare needed new tools to convince an established and successful sales team that the competitive environment was changing and that more could be achieved:

One sticking point was getting the customer-facing teams to deliver the change. Our industry has been stuck doing what it does in the way it does for forever and a day. The response has always been, 'We have experts who do this, so why would they change their approach?'. However, of the customer audience who could move into retirement housing, only 2 per cent currently do. So, what about the other 98 per cent... why not? This was how we started to unstick one of our key challenges – getting our people to believe. How? Embed. Embed. Embed.

Remember that we're often asking customers to commit to residential sites in their town before they've been built. We can show them pictures of what buildings and apartments will look like – but our competitors can do that too. It's much harder to communicate the services and service we provide – to show what it will actually be like to live in one of our residences. We needed to get our sales people to believe before they could get our customers to.

We designed and delivered master classes for our sales teams to help them understand the service and experience of living in a Pegasus property. We focused on the art of building relationships and becoming an expert storyteller. We showed that the tools of sales collateral, brochures, floor plans and so on would only take us so far. We had to help sales teams understand our audience better and help them see our product through the lens of our customer, not ours. We built an experience showroom on the high street of one town we were building in so that people could have a taste of the experience of being a resident. We've created 'taster' apartments in some of our residences so that potential customers can have an even more immersive experience and try before they buy.

The Customer Journey Map we created is built into our induction for new recruits – no matter which part of the business you work in, you will get to walk through the end-to-end purchase and ownership customer journey as we intend it to be.

Our biggest challenge was to ensure the business's daily emergencies didn't stop us from sticking to and investing in the plan. 'Project Engine' now has a monthly slot into which all the work in the business that impacts how we sell flows. We keep board presence at the sessions and reference the vision we created with Engine through daily language and in project. This way it stays alive in our minds.

Keep your customers represented in the design process

In all this project management activity, it can be surprisingly easy to forget about the very people you're doing this for: your customers. So you'll need to bring the internal conversation back to them on a regular basis.

One of the issues you'll probably come across is that of discussions tending to return to what the business wants and can deliver, rather than what your customers actually desire. This is why it's vital to talk to your customer groups, not just in the planning and research phases, but also when you're coming up with ideas, evaluating them and testing possible solutions. And in the same way, you should involve your frontline colleagues; getting their views and testing their understanding of what you're asking them to deliver will give you a more realistic view of your service. How about bringing both staff and customers into your workshops, or creating a small working group online?

Create an experimental environment and learn through doing

Testing as you go along helps to build confidence and consensus. This means you sometimes need to get up from your desk and physically do things. It might mean working with building blocks and toys, plotting ideas out, role playing with your colleagues, or going out as a team and experiencing a service. In fact, it's surprising how many employees don't experience the very service they're trying to transform or improve. If you work for a mobile phone company, for instance, you probably get a free package from your employer, which means you don't ever have to know what it looks and feels like to pay your bill. You also don't get to experience anyone else's network.

It's both the action of doing, and the attitude of being open to experiences that are outside the way you normally work, that create the right conditions for change. They help you to learn something new and get a fresh perspective on things. Some businesses insist on locking everything down so they know exactly what's going to happen and when. It's up to you to gently push back on this and say, 'We don't know what will happen. By the time we get to this point we might have decided this is completely the wrong tack.' Of course, you may scare some people by suggesting this, but you shouldn't be deciding everything at the beginning just so you feel comfortable. When we feel free to change our minds later on it can lead to amazing results.

Stick with it

Finally, this kind of work requires resilience and perseverance. Your project can't be just one exciting kick-off workshop and then business as usual. It's so easy for that initial energy to dissipate, with the result that you end up holding the same old meetings and writing the same old documents. You just lose it. Having a clear to-market process helps, but you also need to prepare yourself for the long haul ahead. It's okay to stop and reflect. Ensure you're still certain why you're doing this thing, and work to keep the vision feeling real in your own mind.

Here are five questions to check whether you've created the right conditions for your project:

- **Right scope and ambition:** is everyone comfortable that you've defined the project correctly, and have you redefined it if needed?
- **Right people:** have you got the right people with the right skills and mindset engaged on it, and are they motivated enough to commit to a sustained effort?
- **Right communications:** have you made the purpose of your work clear from the start, and are your messages still relevant throughout the design and development process?
- **Right level of flexibility:** have you put the people and governance in place to ensure issues get spotted and shared, and the action needed is made clear?
- **Right support:** are your senior sponsors reporting positively about the progress and benefits of your project?

Key takeaways

- Creating the right internal conditions for your service transformation project to flourish means you can deliver results more quickly and avoid having to justify your vision again and again as time goes by.

- Here's how you know when you've created the right conditions:
  - there's a sense of urgency about delivering that doesn't peter out over time;
  - you find you're able to remove 'blockers' without too much difficulty because everyone is aligned to the vision;
  - your colleagues want to be a part of the project and it attracts resources relatively easily;
  - you receive positive feedback both internally from colleagues and externally from customers, who appreciate the quick wins you've delivered.

- Setting and sustaining the right conditions involves:
  - gathering a core group of motivated people at the heart of your project who will remain committed come what may;
  - ensuring this group has sufficient mental and physical resources throughout the project's lifecycle;
  - being prepared to collaborate with teams around the business;
  - giving the people involved good reasons to believe in the vision, and convince those who are reluctant to see the need for it;
  - not forgetting your customers in all this – keep talking to them;
  - adopting an experimental approach so you keep learning by doing without feeling too uncomfortable with uncertainty;
  - developing the resilience to see it through to the end.

References

Kotter, J P (2007) Leading change: Why transformation efforts fail, *Harvard Business Review*, January

Kotter, J P (2014) *Accelerate: Building strategic agility for a faster-moving world*, Harvard Business Review Press, Boston, MA

Run engaging projects 12

Let's face it, your organization is crammed full of projects – it seems as if everyone's got one on the go. This means that if yours is to attract the best people and resources, it needs to stand out as being the most engaging and exciting one to work on. So what would motivate people to turn up to your workshop rather than someone else's, or to commit their freshest ideas and highest energies to your plans? And once you've got these colleagues on board, how will you keep them interested for as long as it takes?

Over the years, we've developed some specialized tools and original ways of thinking about how to set up and run projects that our clients find inspiring. We've learned that in large and small organizations, significant, transformative projects need to be thought of as having their own customer value proposition. In other words, you need to put thought into how the people you need to get involved in your project will need to understand it in order to see it as worthwhile. The benefits of committing to your project will need to be clear for those individuals involved and for the organization, perhaps in the form of new tools and skills developed on the project or new ways of measuring effectiveness that can be applied elsewhere. And when you think about your project as an internal proposition to your business, why not give it a brand and market it as though it were a product? Why not think about delivering a great experience of working on your project to those involved?

In this chapter we'll briefly propose why we think projects that are engaging (and more so than others in play) get better results. We'll also set out nine tactics to consider when you're setting up and running your project to help ensure you have the right people and resources on your side.

Why is it so important for your project to be engaging and enjoyable to work on?

This might seem fairly obvious – everyone wants to have fun, right? That's certainly true, but the benefits you'll get from running an engaging project go further than that. Doing so can help you:

- get more from the people working on the project;
- have better ideas;
- get ideas and solutions from people who don't normally contribute;
- take the burden off senior decision-makers;
- unlock resources and encourage other projects and teams to align with yours.

We'll expand on each of these in brief.

You get more from the people working on the project

When you're guiding a group of colleagues through a service design and development process, your likelihood of success is stronger when the people doing the work are enjoying themselves. So where does this enjoyment come from? It can be through bringing originality to the tasks they do, the chance for them to exercise new skills and, frankly, a dose of fun. Helping our clients run engaging projects for many years has taught us something invaluable: when people start working in a different way with new tools, they gain new perspectives and it always produces more exciting outcomes.

You have better ideas

If you make your project the one people want to work on, you'll attract colleagues to it who want to contribute their views and expertise. It is better still if you can convince managers to release the best from your frontline teams so they can be involved too. And it's even better still if you can co-opt some customers into your design team, through workshops and events, or interviews and working sessions with them in their homes, workplaces or online. It continues to surprise us how much we don't know, and how many ideas we don't see, until we spend time with the right people.

You get ideas and solutions from people who don't normally contribute

A design-led approach to service development thrives on collaboration both vertically and horizontally in your organization. This benefits you in three ways:

- through increased awareness and buy-in (which reduces blockages down the line);

- through the robustness of the thinking you get when you make contact with a broad range of colleagues and customers (which enables better decision-making);

- through the distribution of the burden of decision-making to the teams, customers, and to the process of design itself (for example, through collaborative evaluation techniques and prototyping).

In other words, when your project is enjoyable and rewarding to work on, you'll attract a wider circle of people with more diverse experiences, which means you'll get superior results more quickly.

You take the burden off senior decision-makers

Those who are senior in an organization often feel the weight of leadership. They're expected to have all the brightest ideas, and are sometimes seen as an oracle when it comes to decision-making. But although the final call comes down to them, one person can never have all the answers. The more strategic and forward-looking your project is, the higher the stakes when it comes to decision-making, and the greater the pressure on those at the top. With this comes the possibility that they'll default to 'no' if they're not able to understand what they're being asked to sign off and, if they don't feel enough confidence in your solution to own the risk, a 'no' is understandable.

Many senior decision-makers gain that confidence from data on the performance of existing solutions. Such historical data is useful for modelling future performance and assessing a likely return when the changes being made are incremental and the feedback loop is short. But it's much harder to make a case based on historical data for proposals to make significant changes to your customer proposition and experience – in other words, to create something new. Historical and trend data can still be patched together to give approximate predictions, but in these cases decision-makers need other forms of evidence. These decisions will feel more like those of a venture capitalist than a traditional manager, and your senior managers may need help to think like venture capitalists.

People invest in people, so you need to assemble a group of influencers and delivery people worthy of investment. Hence you need your project to engage the right expertise. Your senior stakeholders will need to feel comfortable with the process you've been through, the rigour of the insights you've gathered through working with customers, and the experts you've brought on board. Engaging influencers in and around your organization provides a powerful social proof as evidence of the validity of your designed vision and plan for change.

You unlock resources and encourage other projects and teams to align with yours

At any moment there may be other projects and teams that are also improving services in your organization. They're probably widely scattered and not necessarily aware of what the others are doing. If their activities were aligned with your own overarching project that would make a lot of sense, but to do this they first need to know about what you're planning, and secondly need to have enough confidence in it to come on board. What you need is social influence.

Here's where positive feedback from senior influencers and budget holders comes in. An engaging project that proves its value early on by attracting the time and resources of the right people will generate this kind of attention. This becomes the social proof of the value of the project, giving others around the business the confidence to commit. In essence, success breeds success.

How can you make your project the project people want to work on?

There is much you can do to make your projects engaging to work on. Here are some suggestions:

- Engage expertise ahead of time.
- Create an engagement plan and think about how and when to involve key people.
- Think about what will motivate individuals and teams to be involved.
- Link your project to the most pressing challenges and questions in your business.
- Create a story and build a brand for your project.
- Make your project visible and accessible so the organization is clear what's going on.
- Get people out of the office and into the world.
- Match the right people to the right parts of the process.
- Make your project in some way a first.

Engage expertise ahead of time

Although it's not good to determine all your solutions at the start, it's useful to play out the work ahead of time and identify what the content of your project is likely to be. For example, you may anticipate that you'll need to understand more about how a particular aspect of your customer operation works, or that you'll want data that your Insight team doesn't routinely gather. You're likely to need help pulling the numbers together so that you can model the cost of operating your current solution and the commercial benefits of redesigning it. Think about what might come up, and start gathering the expertise ahead of time. Getting input from acknowledged experts in and outside your organization will make the project more interesting for everyone, as you'll all learn something new.

Create an engagement plan and think about how and when to involve key people

Think about the people you need to involve directly in the work, and those who only need to be kept in the loop. Plan how you'll work with each person. Find out how they like to receive information, how much hands-on contact they want and how often, remembering that not everybody needs to be involved in every step. The best way to engage senior people might not be to invite them to every workshop, but to take time to ensure they're happy with what's going on. Be clear about the difference between a workshop and a presentation, and don't waste people's time in a workshop by bringing one stakeholder up to speed. Equally, don't expect senior people to contribute freely if they've not been part of the project for several weeks or months, as they're more likely to challenge and ask questions.

Think about what will motivate individuals and teams to be involved

Like it or not, we're all drawn to the fun and interesting stuff in life. As we mentioned earlier, your project will be one of many competing for people's attention and resources. Their commitment will come down to the intrinsic rewards they get from being involved. Although everyone is motivated by different things, the work should feel purposeful and rewarding in some way for everyone involved. This doesn't mean it *always* has to be fun, although it's even better if it is!

Successful projects have a small number of people at the centre who 'get it', want to commit their time, and will tap in to their networks for support. They're personally motivated to commit effort, and are likely to predict that a positive outcome will personally benefit them in some way. Beyond this core, your wider team also needs to feel motivated. This group may not anticipate job promotions and accolades, but they'll be drawn to work that gives them a chance to demonstrate their expertise, learn new skills, or work in a new way with different people.

Remember, you'll need to be crystal clear about what you need from others. They probably can't guess, and if they're not sure, they'll be nervous about committing themselves or their resources. A project with a great story behind it and that seems to be gaining attention and traction will attract people and resources.

Link your project to the most pressing challenges and questions in your business

All organizations have issues, but some are more profound than others. What are the thorny problems for your company related to financial performance, your customers, or both? And how can you link your project to them in such a way that it presents a credible solution to at least one of them?

This depends not only on you identifying the right problem to start off with, but also on how you talk about it. So often, projects are planned and discussed in ways that don't relate to the central issues. For instance, you might identify a business problem to do with finding ways of serving a new type of customer entering your marketplace, which leads you to establish an initiative to transform your company website. So far so good, but you'll need to ensure everybody is clear on the purpose and benefits of your project; it can't be understood only as a technical challenge or a visual refresh.

To secure the permissions and resources you'll need, your project must appeal to the objectives of the right people in senior roles. For example, by aligning your web project with a planned brand repositioning, or identifying it as an opportunity to pilot an omnichannel customer proposition, you'll start to grow its senior network outside your own area. Think about whose attention and resources you need in order to ensure your proposed solution is woven into the objectives of the rest of the business. Doing this doesn't mean overstepping your remit, it simply ensures everybody is clear that your project, however lowly, has value. Importantly, be specific about the KPIs you think you can affect.

Create a story and build a brand for your project

Organizations can have short attention spans, so thinking about how to keep people engaged is a key element of any successful project. Putting something in an email that doesn't get read, or posting an uninspiring update on the company intranet, is usually not enough. Instead, think about how you might make your project feel different from business as usual. One project team we worked with took a 'guerrilla marketing' approach to communication, putting up posters with cryptic images and messages around their offices. This was intriguing and their colleagues wanted to find out more.

As Stella Sangok from the Hyundai Motor Company describes:

> *It's important to look for ways to make the process and communication of the final design attractive and even playful, so people want to engage and understand. In Korea, Service Design is still fairly new. Businesses are focused on understanding and evaluating the theory. Attractive and playful ways of explaining the design process, the vision and the design of the service are very important.*

Think about the communication channels already available to you in your workplace. They may be your departmental weekly stand-ups to update people, ask questions, and get input, or they might be internal social networking tools. Try to get yourself inserted into your internal communications system, whether that is a weekly bulletin or your monthly staff magazine, so you can build the brand around your project.

Having an internal brand for your venture makes it easier for people to talk about it, which means it'll become more widely known throughout your organization. To create a brand, you'll need a project proposition or problem statement. Capture the essence of what you're setting out to achieve, and for whom. To make your project sound appealing, and to ensure it's not confused with others that sound similar, be clear how your approach will get you the outcome you need.

Make your project visible and accessible so the organization is clear what's going on

If at all possible, see if you can own a space in your office from which to run your project for its duration, and use the walls to make your thinking visible. Work there and invite your teams to do the same, bringing stakeholders into the space both formally and informally. Consider making it 'open house', and encourage people to drop by so you can take them through your process and plans. Ensure everybody in the business knows what you're up to, so false rumours don't arise (unless of course your project is top secret!). This collective involvement in proposition and service design can surface and inspire better ideas but it can also begin the process of moving the vision out into the organization and set the stage for implementation.

Get people out of the office and into the world

Get out of your office as much as you can. Go and gather inspiration from your customers' world and from other businesses and services that provide similar experiences or solve similar problems. For example, if what you're designing will require customers to wait in an unavoidable queue, go find some queues to join. Find some great queuing experiences and some terrible ones and discuss why they make you feel the way they do. Be specific: what is it about the design of the service and interactions that produces a great or terrible experience?

Locating some or all of your project in a place other than your head-quarters is ideal. It's a luxury, but consider hiring a very different kind of space, at least for important workshops. Look for a spot that gets you closer to your customers; this could be one of your own retail stores or contact centres, or it could be an external venue. Often, being somewhere different frees up your thinking and gives the team unspoken permission to pose chal-lenges and bring in ideas from the outside world. Getting out of the office is also a brilliant way to get into your customers' world. Find ways to be with them where they are, not where you are.

Match the right people to the right parts of the process

Managing the politics of a group of stakeholders is vital to the success of a project, but it can also hinder it. Our clients often focus too much on the need to engage their senior stakeholders, rather than on how to get the right people in the right room at the right time.

Separated by 10 years, two mathematicians published competing papers arguing whether diverse teams of people, rather than highly able teams, perform better when it comes to solving problems. In other words, whether it's better to get your most skilled people in a room (Thompson, 2014) or to find a group that brings diverse experiences, perspectives and tools to the project (Hong and Page, 2004). In our experience, you need diversity in the early stages of a project, with a team that's not dominated by seniority. This is not the moment for personal visions, closed assumptions or a brief history of everything that's been tried and failed before. Once it comes to moving from vision into planning, that's when you need seniority and delivery expertise. You'll also need design and delivery specialists when you get into crafting the experiences your customers will see, touch and use.

Not all the workshops you'll organize require the same profile of attendees. In particular, avoid (if you can) inviting your most senior stakeholders to creative sessions unless they are genuinely creative, and holding sessions in which rolling up your sleeves and getting into detail is important. Treat stakeholder management and service design as two separate activities, and carefully manage the moments when they coincide.

Make your project in some way a first

Many corporations have adopted a certain project management style, often enforced by a Project Management Office. Although it can be helpful to have some guidance, an imposed style can become tedious and repetitive – it's never inspiring to feel you're just going through the motions. If you can find two or three ways of working that will be recognized as new and unconventional within your company, you'll draw in the right rather than the wrong people.

Remember when we talked about new services being more attractive to your customers when they incorporate a level of novelty or originality? It's the same with your project internally. People are drawn to a venture that doesn't seem to be a re-hash of the 'same old, same old' methods. What's more, the kind of people you want to attract are those who like to do something novel; you'll be encouraging self-selection when they see that there's an opportunity to learn a new skill or make their week more exciting by doing things in a special way.

So how do you go about this? You could put on project events in which you agree how you're going to work. You could go out as a group to experience your competitors' services. You could even bring your customers into one of your workshops, along with your frontline colleagues, and design new services together. Once you challenge yourself to identify some points for newness in your project process, there are no limits to the ideas you can come up with.

Part of the originality of your project will come from bringing the outside in. This could involve inviting your customers into your offices to talk to you, or going out into the outside world and bringing elements of it into your project. It's easy to spend hours poring over charts and data from research agencies, rather than experiencing your services for yourselves or conversing with your own customers face to face. In fact, a lot of people we work with virtually never speak to their own customers. When they do, they find it fascinating and it gives them a new impetus to do good work. This is because by understanding our customers better, we feel more motivated to improve things for them; they've become real people rather than a set of numbers. In fact, much of the value we bring to our clients is in designing these 'outside in' moments, by planning workshops with interesting activities and orchestrating conversations with customers. It makes a huge difference when you're able to see things from a fresh perspective.

Here are five questions to check whether your project is the one that's drawing people in:

1 **Excitement:** do people feel revved up about starting your project?

2 **Early feedback:** is it good, and are senior people talking about your project?

3 **Time:** are people, including the sceptics, making time to take part?

4 **New inputs:** are you attracting new inputs and requests for help from others throughout your organization?

5 **Attraction:** do other areas of your business want to learn from what you're doing?

Key takeaways

- Your project needs to be engaging to work on, because:
  - people give more to something they enjoy;
  - they'll contribute more and better ideas;
  - you'll attract a wider circle than normal, with more diversity of experience;
  - senior decision-makers will feel comfortable with supporting it due to the social proof it has;
  - other teams around the business are likely to notice what you're doing and add their synergy and value to it.
- How do you make your project engaging to work on? You:
  - attract and involve the experts you need ahead of time, as their input will make it more interesting and credible for everyone;
  - get the right people involved in the right way and at the right times;

- work out what will motivate different people to become involved, which is most likely the chance to learn new skills, work in new ways and demonstrate their expertise;

- identify how it helps your business with its most pressing problems, and talk about it as such;

- create a story and brand identity for it and use the most appropriate communication channels to showcase them;

- create, if you can, an internal space for people to 'visit' so they can see what's going on;

- keep in touch with your customers' world and learn from other companies doing the same thing, by getting out of the office and into the customer space;

- treat your senior stakeholders differently from the other people involved, so each person is engaged with the right part of the process;

- bring originality into the way you run it by doing things differently from the way they're normally done, especially when it comes to spending time with your customers.

References

Hong, L and Page, S E (2004) Groups of diverse problem solvers can outperform groups of high-ability problem solvers, *Proceedings of the National Academy of Sciences of the United States of America*, **101** (46), pp 16,385–89

Thompson, A (2014) Does diversity trump ability? An example of the misuse of mathematics in the social sciences, *Notices of the American Mathematical Society*, **61** (9), pp 1024–30

Think like
a Designer

13

'Some people think design means how it looks. But of course, if you dig deeper, it's really how it works.'

STEVE JOBS, FORMER CEO, APPLE (WOLF, 1996)

Imagine you need a lawyer to help you sell your house. Unsure where to start, you'd probably check out a few websites offering conveyancing services. They all seem to offer similar services to a competent standard, but you get a very different feeling about each company from the experience of using their websites. Some are crammed with jargon-filled text and poor-quality images, with information that's both hard to find and understand, while others seem to have had time and money invested in the design and the words. Which would you put on your shortlist?

The truth is that people are attracted to well-designed things, valuing them more than poorly designed ones. But, as Steve Jobs clearly understood, design is about more than how something looks. It's even about more than how something works. Design (with a capital 'D') is as much about a process as it is about a product. It's a way of thinking and working; importantly, it's an attitude that says, 'How can we make this thing the best it can be?'

Market-leading businesses have seen the value of what we've referred to throughout this book as 'design thinking', and of changing their organization by first re-imagining the products and services they should deliver and then re-organizing with a goal to deliver them; what we call 'design-led change'. Business and management schools have been studying Designers and their approaches for at least the last decade, and incorporating them into approaches to running businesses. In an interview in 2017, Matt Candy, Vice President of IBM iX, told the UK Design Council, 'Design thinking is the science of the 21st century so using that approach for problem solving is the way in which businesses will reinvent themselves' (Times Higher Education, 2017).

In his book *The Design of Business*, Roger Martin (formerly the Dean of the Rotman School of Management at the University of Toronto) points out that, although the design process and design thinking aren't right for every problem a business faces, 'When your challenge is to create value or seize an emerging opportunity, the solution is to perform like a design team: work iteratively, build a prototype, elicit feedback, refine it, and repeat. Give yourself a chance to uncover problems and fix them in real time, as the process unfolds' (Martin, 2009: 121).

We've titled this chapter 'Think like a Designer' because we, your authors, are Designers. What we have in common is that we're design school graduates, which gives us specific training and experience in combining arts and engineering. And it's our belief, the founding belief of Engine in fact, that trained Designers have something to offer beyond the roles traditionally given to Designers within many of the organizations we work with. We use a capital 'D' when we talk about Designers who went to design school, but the good news is you don't have to go back to college to think like a Designer.

You may have some design school-trained Designers in your organization. You may have departments full of them. They may be digital designers, graphic designers, interior designers or product designers by training. It's most likely they're employed to give form, colour and structure to things your customers come into contact with. But whatever their role, we're sure some of these Designers will be wired in ways that mean they can contribute more strategically to the success of your business.

In this chapter, we'll make the case for design school-trained Designers and the ways they (we) think and work. Although the skills of trained Designers are not unique, Designers embody thinking and working styles that are increasingly relevant to businesses. We'll explain what we think these are and how – without going to design school – you and your team can think and work more like Designers.

All we ask is that you:

- embrace and understand Design as being about more than how things look;

- adopt some thinking habits of Designers to give yourself an edge;

- seek out the Designers in your organization and put them to work in supporting you to make change happen.

Before we go further, let's get clear on the difference between an *output* and designing a service to realize an *outcome*. An output is a tangible element of your project process (such as those we described in Chapter 10), for example, a Customer Journey Map, Service Blueprint or Service Flatplan, or eventually a customer website, an app or plans for a new store interior. An outcome, on the other hand, is defined by the benefits you'll achieve, such as more loyal customers, an improved company reputation or happier colleagues. Of course, the outcomes are what your project is really about. However, if you invest in the design and quality of your outputs, you're more likely to achieve the outcomes you want. After all, whether we are colleagues or customers, we're all people responding emotionally to what's put in front of us. So 'good design' is an important factor in the success of your venture well before your customers get to see or use anything new. It's important right from the initiation of your project and the conception of your vision for how things can be better.

Why is it important to think like a Designer?

It's important to get your Designer head on, because when you have, you'll:

- find it easier to imagine fresh solutions;
- be able to think visually;
- be more likely to think ahead;
- have more ideas;
- be able to make your ideas tangible;
- have an insatiable appetite for improvement;
- see constraints as a source of inspiration;
- create unique, protectable solutions.

Let's briefly expand on each of these:

Designers are great at imagining how others will experience and interpret solutions

Designers are interested in how things work and how they can be more usable, useful and desirable. They're always looking for ways to make what they're designing better, and this is driven from an optimistic view of the future. They also ask lots of questions about why something is as it is, such as 'what if?' or 'why can't we?', because questioning why something works a certain way can lead to revealing answers. This is born from a curiosity about the things around us, which might be innate but is not unique to design-school types. You can do it too.

Designers are good at the 'so what's?', too. Sometimes it's easier to highlight issues than it is to imagine solutions, or even to imagine that new solutions might exist. Thinking like a Designer means feeling free to combine seemingly unrelated observations and examples to build a new picture of how things work today, to test unlikely hypotheses casually in conversation without fear of looking stupid, and to imagine novel combinations of existing solutions.

Designers are trained to think and communicate visually

Designers think visually. They analyse information in this way and use visualization to communicate problems, information, frameworks of thought and new solutions. A large part of the design process involves 'selling an idea' (or a problem) to others – what we often describe as 'bridging the imagination gap'. Simple visualizations can cut through subjective discussions and make new ideas unambiguous. Visualization also helps people believe in the possible, because there's something about making an idea visual that removes uncertainty.

It's important to appreciate that getting visual isn't only about making your work more interesting and appealing to look at. Visual thinking is a psychological phenomenon. Design schools may attract more than their fair share of visual thinkers, and if you're not one of them don't worry, it's likely that several of your colleagues are.

Designers like to be part of the latest thing

Designers are drawn to newness and always have one eye on the future, which is a great place to look for inspiration about what can be made better today. Through understanding the technological, social and behavioural landscape for your customer, they're in tune with the changes that need to be made. The future often happens sooner than we think, so it's helpful to have a few people around you who make it their business to be part of it first.

Designers like to know a little bit about a lot of things

Traditionally, professionals are valued because of their specialism and deep expertise. Today, generalism has become a prized specialism. The ability to facilitate multidisciplinary teams, to understand just enough across a breadth of subject areas and to make creative connections, borrowing solutions from other domains, is highly valued. Designers structure their work fully around projects as opposed to formal roles, responsibilities or business objectives: 'The typical designer's resume consists of an accumulation of projects rather than an accumulation of hierarchical job titles. The project-based approach informs the entire mindset of the designer' (Martin, 2009: 119). Designers are motivated more by a great culture and exciting work than the prospect of promotion. This diversity of experience makes them great at creativity because they can draw on diverse experiences. Project-working naturally focuses them on a collective rather than individual goals.

Designers make things tangible as soon as possible, so they can learn from doing so

Making something isn't just what happens at the end of the project; it's part of the design process itself. Design can feel a bit like science in this regard, in that reaching a new product or service through experimentation, rather than by working with historical assumptions or beliefs, will result in a better solution.

If a picture paints a thousand words, then a prototype simply doesn't shut up. Being able to experience something early, even in a very basic and unrefined form, reveals lessons you'd never learn on paper. Designers are always making ideas visual and tangible because the act of doing so moves their thinking forward. Prototyping doesn't have to be big and expensive. Sketching, role-play and building with LEGO® are all ways to learn through making.

As your project progresses, your solutions will become clearer and your prototypes more real and elaborate. Digital products and experiences can be prototyped and shared in a matter of minutes or a few hours. We've proto-typed physical services at scale using IKEA furniture, with real customers and even professional actors, who are great at getting into character and assum-ing the manner of different types of customer. We've prototyped an improved experience for airport passengers travelling through security checks and immigration. We've prototyped the experience for customers checking out at a supermarket using a mobile app on their phone to scan goods so they can jump the checkout queues. We've built a car dealership at full scale (again using IKEA furniture and cardboard) so that we can experiment with staff roles and behaviours as well as new digital sales tools with customers.

Designers will keep improving something until they're told to stop

Rarely are the best ideas the ones you come up with first time around. They're the product of several iterations of an idea, tweaked and developed, tested and enhanced repeatedly. Designers naturally get into the detail sooner rather than later, and keep asking questions about how the process and the product could be improved. Their ambition is to challenge their own assumptions until the solution is as good as they can make it, or someone tells them to stop.

Designers relish a challenge and see constraints as a source of inspiration

It's hard to imagine how constraints can be inspiring, but it is possible to see how people can be energized by the idea of finding an elegant solution when there are so many factors to take into consideration. It's a form of negotiation with the objective to get to a better than expected outcome with the least compromise. Marty Neumeier makes the same point more boldly in his book, *The Designful Company*, saying, 'Designful leaders don't accept the hand-me-down notion that cost-cutting and innovation are mutually exclusive, or that short-term and long-term goals are irreconcilable. They reject the tyranny of "or" in favour of the genius of "and"' (Neumeier, 2009: 47).

Great design is hard to copy

LEGO® is famous for the clarity of its model instructions, managing to achieve this with almost no written language at all. It makes it look easy, but it's not. We've all experienced the flatpack furniture nightmare of incomprehensible directions, leaving us frustrated and confused as we try to match side A with shelf B, but LEGO® does it so much better.

LEGO® has been a design-led organization right from the beginning, investing in design and having a culture that respects it all the way through. This is how it's created a market-leading product that is so hard to copy.

'Good execution provides its own obstacles to imitation because it is difficult to achieve' (Lanning and Michaels, 1988). If something is well made, it's incredibly hard to copy. A precision-engineered Swiss watch, for instance, has a depth of quality that comes from how it's put together as much as what it looks like; as a result, it can multiply its value over the years and even become an heirloom. The same applies to a service or customer experience. You can tell your frontline staff to smile and say 'Have a nice day', but if the underlying systems and culture don't support them, customers will sense that the feeling isn't genuine. Achieving quality starts with the very nature of the design process you follow.

What's worth designing well?

Good design should run through your entire project process, from the creation of initial concepts through to the materials you use to communicate them with others, and to the elements of your new service. So if designing isn't only about what happens right at the end, where else can good or indeed great design enhance your project and make it more successful?

There are various areas in which design plays a critical part in service development:

- in the materials you create to make your case;
- in the tools you use to understand your customer experience;
- in the materials you use to test solutions and mobilize teams;
- in the things your customers use.

The things you create to make the case for addressing an issue or opportunity

Here are some examples of what you can design in order to make the case for your proposed solution:

- simple and well-designed information graphics showing key data as evidence for change;
- presentations and movies showing senior stakeholders what the experience feels like for your customers and colleagues today;
- the design of a real-world experience, walking in your customers' shoes;
- a show-reel of your competitors' services;
- a storyboard showing how your customers will experience your new service;
- digital prototypes of your new website or mobile app.

The tools to understand your customer experience and imagine a new one

There are many ways you can visualize how your customer experience works or will work. Here are some examples:

- a long poster showing your current customer journey, highlighting their pain-points along with opportunities to improve it;

- a visualization of your current service ecosystem, showing all the 'actors' in it: the people, roles, and other services that have an impact on how your customers buy and use your services and the relationships between them;

- mood boards and visual inspiration from your industry that gets colleagues excited about what's possible, and what's already shaping your customers' expectations;

- sketches and storyboards that help people imagine how new ideas will play out for customers;

- posters or life-size standing banners depicting fictional customer personas, representing the customer groups you're designing for.

Materials to test solutions and mobilize teams

What could you create in order to prototype and test your proposed solutions? Here are some ideas:

- paper and digital mock-ups of imagined customer touchpoints you can put in front of customers and colleagues to gauge their reactions;

- mock-ups of customer communications to test your marketing messages;

- handbooks for communicating with your colleagues involved in the pilot (these should explain why the pilot is happening, what's being piloted and how, and how they can give feedback);

- training materials for frontline staff;

- clear reporting documentation.

The things your customers and colleagues touch and use

Let's not forget the actual service itself. Here's a selection of what could be included here:

- the digital user experience and visual design;

- the design of the physical products your customers buy or use;

- physical spaces;

- communications;

- customer service roles and conversations (yes, conversations can be designed too);

- uniforms;
- visual branding.

How can you start to think and work like a Designer?

You don't have to enrol at design school, nor do Designers have a monopoly on empathy, curiosity, creativity, ingenuity or a knack for detail. However, having spent 40 years between the three of us inside companies of all sizes, we've observed people's reactions to how we think and work, and have had some great conversations with some enthusiastic advocates of design thinking as a result.

Here are some tips on Designer habits to adopt, all of them gleaned from 'non-Designers'. They offer insights into how others see the value of Designers, and in summary, are:

- being prepared to take enough time;
- trusting the design process;
- valuing insight more than data;
- communicating visually;
- being ready to start making;
- developing design thinking skills.

Defend the time you need to have ideas and evolve them

The solution you'll develop and deploy might not be something you've imagined yet. If your business genuinely wants to create something new and sees the commercial value in doing it well, you'll need to allow enough time.

In Chapter 3, 'The challenge of fast and slow', we discussed how difficult it can be to balance the conflicting needs of making change happen quickly and of doing the forward planning that allows longer-term investment decisions to be made. In projects and programmes, there's always a pressure to progress to the next stage. Agile development has challenged this traditional waterfall approach by assembling multidisciplinary teams and working in short, iterative cycles. Yet agile suits product development much better than service initiatives impacting large numbers of people and many systems at once. For these projects, allowing enough time to explore the issues, gain formative insights and experiment remains important. So you'll need to make the case early on for protecting your time and resist the temptation to promise you can deliver an impactful solution overnight.

The best way to run out of time, by the way, is to start too late. Encourage senior stakeholders to initiate projects quickly, resource them well enough, remove the blockers, and be prepared to sign off next stages and budgets as soon as they are needed.

Trust the design process

Designers are trained in the 'design process'. In simple terms, this is: understanding the problem or need, knowing who you're designing for, having a load of ideas, picking the best ones, prototyping them as much as you can, refining one design, detailing it, and making it real. This isn't always how businesses work, and nor do they have to for every purpose. But for your objective of creating a new customer experience they do. Although some steps can be completed in days, not weeks or months, make sure you work through the process and don't skip any steps.

Figure 13.1   When we are working with clients we sit the simple logical steps of the design process into a broader project or programme structure

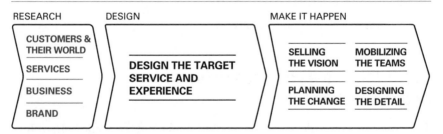

RESEARCH

CUSTOMERS & THEIR WORLD

SERVICES

BUSINESS

BRAND

DESIGN

DESIGN THE TARGET SERVICE AND EXPERIENCE

MAKE IT HAPPEN

SELLING THE VISION

PLANNING THE CHANGE

MOBILIZING THE TEAMS

DESIGNING THE DETAIL

Value insight over data

Insights help to define a problem statement or commercial opportunity or to inspire a solution. Having one or two at the centre of your project story can be a powerful thing, particularly if it relates to some fundamental truth about human behaviour, what motivates your customers, or about your business.

The definition of 'an insight' is hard to pin down but, importantly, it's not the same thing as data, an observation or common knowledge. An insight is a realization about the world. It's something you couldn't have known until

Table 13.1 The service design process can be described with a simple set of logical steps

1	2	3	4	5	6	7
Get informed and inspired by your customers.	Explore customer problems and needs widely to reduce the chance of missing something valuable.	Imagine many possible solutions.	Collaborate to prioritize with a clear understanding of how value will be realized for your customers and your business.	Design and evaluate solutions by starting with how customers will experience them (not how you'll deliver within your current operation).	Use this target customer experience to determine change requirements.	Place the target experience at the end of the roadmap and work backwards to determine what to do first and what to start working towards.

you engaged with the world or data about the world. Getting an insight is having a moment of realization, so in that sense you must work at it. The insights you generate and use when you analyse data or spend time with your customers may not be original to the world, but they ought to bring something original to your project. You can build complete propositions around a great insight, and having some and being able to provide evidence for them can give the sceptics reasons to believe.

Trained Designers are useful people when it comes to revealing insights because they are naturally both curious and empathetic. They like to figure out what makes people and the world tick. They look at data and try to imagine the people from whom the data was generated. They ask 'why?'

So let's briefly illustrate the difference between using customer data to inform action and using an insight. We return to our fictional business, Bermondsey Health Insurance International. They had their corporate objectives, their mission statement and their corporate strapline but none of these really helped to focus the organization on the proposition their customers would really value, or the service they needed to design.

So, they did what came naturally to them, which was to review their customer data. They had a lot of data from customer satisfaction surveys and sales figures and it told them that their customers were least satisfied by the speed of the insurance claims process. This led to the suggestion that they should build their vision for their service around 'speed' and 'ease'.

Then one executive suggested that they should all go and spend some time with their member customers, and just talk to them. They did, and they did hear many customers complain about the speed at which claims were processed and how many of them would like a more personal service. But they also heard their customers' experiences of travelling to work in another country, of making that decision, of ensuring their families back home were reassured and would be looked after, of needing to research how they could get their regular medication in the country they were travelling to and access medical care. What they saw was that their customers were ambitious and adventurous; they were people who wanted to advance their careers and earn more by making a move overseas. The team also realized (the insight) that for their customers to focus on their work and careers meant not having to worry about their health. This insight became central to how the business developed its products and services and how it communicated with its customers.

Communicate visually (or find someone who can)

You'll encourage more people to believe in your project internally if your tangible outputs look good and are easy to understand. For instance, telling a story about why your service needs to change through a storyboard or a movie will communicate it in a more compelling way than simply listing a set of process steps. You could say beautifully designed communications are superficial, but the fact is, they work. We see this with our clients. Sometimes they create their own internal documents on the fly, with disappointing results for them. When we design beautifully persuasive visuals for them, this can unlock internal resources they never dreamed of.

But this is about more than just influence. Having well-designed information internally means people are more likely to grasp what your customer issues are in the first place, or understand what your group as a business will go on to build. Clearly and persuasively presented information at the *ready-to-build* phase (see Chapter 10) will ensure the people who'll be figuring out how to make your service work are super clear on what they need to produce; you're removing the 'lost in translation' problem through great information design.

You might have a graphic design or marketing department, but may not have considered using the Designers in it to make your transformational project or the ways you communicate operational information more successful. Some of the companies we work with are starting to build bridges with the more creative parts of their business, not in the conventional way, but by seeing design skills as having a role internally and as part of delivering change.

Assemble a toolkit

It's possible that you're already using some or all of the tools that we use with our clients every day to imagine, prototype and deploy new services and customer experiences. The tools are all out there; the effort is in making them your own and getting people to use them. Once we've been working with a business for a while it makes sense to begin to collect together the tools that we've been using and develop a system of assets and templates for our client to use themselves.

We've seen that developing even a basic set of tools helps to establish customer experience design as a 'thing', as a practice within your business and, if you stick with it, to establish and embed a shared vocabulary across the business. As the design of your customer experience becomes even more important to leaders in your organization, the toolkit will be there to ensure that people who don't normally think about what customers experience can work with those who do.

We developed a Customer Experience Toolkit for Samantha and the teams she works with at Transport for London. We developed the toolkit to package up the thinking we developed while working on an experience design project. The toolkit was a by-product of the design project. We asked Sam why it was important to her to have a kit of tools she could reuse:

A [customer experience design] toolkit is a great way of maximizing the value of the investment in a future customer experience design project to build organizational capability beyond the project team. The value is in its delicate balance between theory and practice. The tools Engine design and package – and train us on – helpfully explain the logic and benefits of design-led thinking whilst providing practical tools and techniques to support us to deliver the experience design process ourselves. Someone who is new to customer experience design can pick it up and quickly become confident by understanding the approach and actually applying the tools.

E.ON Energy, a business that we feel has one of the most mature service design practices in-house, has developed a range of tools to be used by teams across the group to support better service and experience design. Some are very simple but powerful nonetheless. Keith told us:

We introduced a checklist to ensure the end-to-end experience was considered right at the start of product development, resulting in much better solutions that performed better for customers. The likelihood of a product failing has decreased because fewer but better products are making it to market. Focusing on 'experience' and not just 'product' makes product development far more efficient.

Develop your design thinking skills

You've possibly had to brief a UX or graphic designer or perhaps an interior designer, and been disappointed with what you got back. This may have been because you didn't have the most useful language or the references to use with him or her at the time. But there's a lot you can do to develop your design vocabulary and critical skills to help you understand your Designer's ideas and thought process, and to more precisely explain to them what you need.

Why not run a Design Thinking immersion day with your team? Take them out to a design museum (or major department store), for instance, and spend the day trying to understand a specific set of questions, such as, 'What is good design?', and 'How do you describe it?'. This will help you to see and articulate an appreciation of what makes design work well. You can also re-read Chapter 8, 'Design your service beautifully'; essentially that's a checklist for how to answer the question, 'Is this thing I'm about to create any good?'

One of the great things E.ON Energy has done to focus the organization on their customers is to address a skills gap head-on and build a service design capability internally. E.ON now has a well-developed service design training programme (based on a design process model we introduced in 2010). As well as the skills developed, this group-wide programme has given the organization a shared vocabulary with which to work and design together and opportunities to share their experiences of designing and delivering for customers. Keith explains how E.ON has used training to help create the conditions for great customer experience design and delivery:

> *We've adopted Design Thinking as our chosen approach to imagining and implementing human-centred solutions regardless of whether we need to improve the experience for customers of commodity energy supply – or we're looking to innovate a new product or service. Colleagues from across the organization are trained in Design Thinking and methods and in particular how to understand what customers – people – need. They learn how to think differently and use this understanding to bring comprehensive solutions to market which really satisfy our customers' needs with speed. Spread across all regions, 1,600 colleagues have attended training so far. We run training in four different languages and there are several examples of how Design Thinking has been put into practice on real projects in the business. The next steps are to demonstrate the impact it has on us as an organization and to develop the programme further to support colleagues to apply the methods and tools they learned to more of what they are doing in their daily work.*

Here are five questions to check whether design is at the heart of your service:

1 **Persuasive:** are your visual communications getting people excited and motivated about your project?

2 **Quality:** is your proposed service transformation grounded in genuine insight?

3 **Branding:** are your activities geared towards creating a set of communications, and a service, which is intrinsically yours?

4 **Innovative:** have you tried novel ways of getting your message across?

5 **Understanding:** do you and the teams working on your project understand what good service design is, and why it's important?

Key takeaways

- Good design is crucial, both when you're creating services that appeal to your customers and when you're winning over your colleagues for your service transformation project.

- Design thinking is about more than looks or even function – it's also about the *process* of developing services your customers will love.

- Thinking like a Designer is important because it will help you to:
  - come up with fresh ideas, rather than rehashing what's already been tried;
  - develop your visualization skills so you're able to win people over more readily;
  - think beyond the horizon to what may be coming up ahead;
  - learn about many areas of your business;
  - make your ideas tangible so everyone can learn from them as quickly as possible;
  - see how you can improve your ideas time and again;
  - rise to challenges with inspired energy;
  - create services that are uniquely yours and are impossible for others to replicate.

- There are many areas in which design plays a critical role in your service transformation project:
  - in the creation of presentation materials to help convince your colleagues of the need for change;
  - in the visualization of how your customers experience your service now and in the future;
  - in the development of materials to prototype and test your ideas;
  - in the design and manufacture of the things your customers will use when the new service is launched.

- Therefore, starting to think like a Designer is an extremely worthwhile process. You can do this by:
  - being prepared to spend enough time, and move with enough speed, to create a quality service solution;
  - trusting the purpose of the design process;

- relying less on research data and a lot more on insights developed through both studying the data and engaging with your customers and their world;

- making great use of your graphic designers to create visually persuasive materials internally;

- starting to 'make' your service early on, rather than leaving it until the end of the process;

- assembling a toolkit to use for future service design projects during the process of your current one;

- developing your design thinking skills by becoming more aware of what great design is and how you can describe it.

References

Lanning, M J and Michaels, E G (1988) A business is a value delivery system, McKinsey Staff Paper No.41, June

Martin, R L (2009) *The Design of Business: Why design thinking is the next competitive advantage*, Harvard Business Press, Boston, MA

Neumeier, M (2009) *The Designful Company: How to build a culture of nonstop innovation*, Peachpit Press, San Francisco, CA

Times Higher Education (2017) IBM and Google on why design graduates are crucial to their industry, 23 October. Available online at: https://www.timeshighereducation.com/student/blogs/ibm-and-google-why-design-graduates-are-crucial-their-industry

Wolf, G (1996) Steve Jobs: The next insanely great thing, *WIRED*, February

Conclusion

By now you'll have a much better understanding of what it takes to become customer-driven as an organization, and get more of the right services to market faster. You'll also have a feel for what makes some organizations so much better at this than others. The empathy to understand their customers, the ambition to create a transformational vision, and the willingness to embrace new attitudes and approaches to project management are all key. Where does your business stand on this? And, just as importantly, where do you?

In the past, it was usual for organizations to get ahead commercially through a combination of marketing spend, operational efficiency and digital transformation. But as you've now seen, there's a limit to what these factors alone can achieve when it comes to creating and delivering superlative services. The imperative that's emerged is to seek ways of innovating to create clear value for both businesses and customers. For this you need a different approach, not just to design and development, but also to the business change needed to deliver it safely to market. Many of our clients have described this as a shift from 'inside out' thinking to 'outside in'. Actually, this is more than simply a change of perspective; it's about designing your organization fully around your customers.

Whatever your experience, the drive to develop new and improved services and customer experiences, and to sell and support them brilliantly, never abates. Moreover, as capabilities develop, you'll find more and more becomes possible. With the constant reinvention of technology and improvements in data gathering, for instance, you can feed your service development process in real time and use the same data to mass-personalize your customers' experiences. However, none of this helps you with these central questions: what will your customers value most over the next couple of years? What will encourage them to notice and buy from you? And how do you deliver your services to them with speed, confidence and quality?

To answer this, your approach needs to move from being led by technology, marketing or resource optimization, to one that's inspired by your customers and led by your vision – with a more experimental and speedy pace than you're probably used to. It should be an approach that uses customer insights to help you create your service proposition, your proposition to inform experience design, and your experience design to tell you what your business must become good at in order to provide a great service. In that order.

This is what we call design-led change. It recognizes that putting something new and of value in your customers' hands isn't just about completing a service development cycle, it's also about inspiring and supporting your organization to invest in and implement it well. There's no two ways about it: great service and experience design is an organizational challenge.

In this book, we've set out and discussed several challenges that we've encountered through our work with all kinds of organizations. It's well understood that to succeed in any business you need to build things your customers will value, yet many organizations still find it hard to organize themselves to do so. Many organizations are great at running the core operations of their business; in fact some are so good – they are optimized so well – that they find it hard to change, even when the need to do so is hard to ignore. And even if the imperative to change is clear and a vision for a future state can be imagined, many organizations struggle with the challenge of translating such a vision into action.

Technology has changed service delivery. Customer service is becoming digitized and personalized customer experiences are being designed and produced in real time. Economics has become much less of an exact science and behavioural economics influences commercial decision-making. Customers' needs and behaviours are diversifying and are hard to predict, and their influence on the prosperity of individual businesses is greater than it's ever been. The need to adapt at pace and on all fronts has sent managers and management consultants looking for new ways to manage. What began as a disruptive idea in software development – The Agile Manifesto – became a mainstream idea in management. Yet the need for speed and the interplay between technology, management and customers has surfaced further challenges.

What is the best approach to managing the need for continual adaptation together with the need for a longer-term investment plan and the very human need for a sense of purpose, a motivating reason to do what you do? And how do you make continual change okay for your customers? Furthermore, as technology makes doing business with a service frictionless, is there a risk that the emotional connection that evidence suggests is one of the reasons customers stay loyal might be lost? In retail banking, utilities, mobile telecoms, media and music services, consumer demand and industry regulation have banished many of the mechanisms businesses used to use to make it hard for customers to leave. Most of these services are now very easy to use. Customer service is automated. Switching is easy. So, the new battleground may be 'emotion' and the ability of businesses to design triggers of positive emotions and a deeper emotional connection into the core of the service proposition and the mechanics of the experience, not just advertising, and to connect with people as people (with complex lives) not just as customers.

As technology makes doing business with any service easier, the need for organizations to signal why they are different becomes important again. 'Easy' is expected, so businesses are seeking points of distinction, of originality (which always has a 'half-life'), and ways of manifesting the values of the brand in both the proposition and the experience.

If you've read this book, chances are you're wrapped up in some or all of these challenges. You're experiencing them in the meetings you're running or sitting in, the papers and presentations you're giving and receiving and in the chatter in meeting pods and break-out spaces. Our vision for this book was as a cross between a management text and a self-help manual. We wanted to write for people like the people we work with every day in the client organizations that commission us (you've heard from some of them too). We wanted to frame the problems as we see them in the hope that we could provide a language with which you can discuss them with your colleagues.

Most importantly, we wanted to make the case for Design (again with a big 'D') and specifically for what's now well known as 'design thinking', an approach not only for getting to better ideas and solutions in the market but to leading change in your organization. This, we appreciate, may be a big conceptual step, so let's circle back around to one of the ideas from the introduction to this book, that services are human systems as much as they are technological ones. So, in essence, if you want to redesign your service and the experience your customers have of it, you often need to 'redesign' the people who'll design, implement and deliver those new solutions. And any sustainable approach to changing and equipping people to perform better and differently involves a developmental journey and exposure to different ideas, heuristics and ways of working. It's in this way that the process of design itself – in the form of a 'design project' – takes a group of people on a developmental journey. After all, people make services for people to use.

So yes, being design-led means that if you follow the right process you'll end up with a better product, and the ways of working that are instilled in big 'D' Designers in design school can help with this. But being design-led is also about considering design thinking and ways of working as a developmental resource for your people too. It can be a practical approach to 'taking people on a journey' that equips them to imagine and then implement a desirable future state, to manage information and uncertainly differently, to envision and craft better solutions and to get more of the right services to market, faster.

'That's all very well,' we can hear you say, 'I get that Design is about more than a better product – it's a mindset and a way of working. And I get that it's important to plan and run a great design project because the project is about more than simply creating a specification and making some decisions – it's about bringing people on the journey, skilling them up and keeping them motivated. But...' you go on to say, '...the organization you're describing here is a million miles away from my organization.'

It's true that when it comes to being customer-centred and design-led, each organization we work with is at a different level of maturity. Those that are furthest to the right on the maturity scale have their problems too. Right now, on their grand journey towards customer-centeredness and being truly adaptive and design-led, these organizations are grappling with four new challenges:

1 Connecting the whole organization, not just the few, to the customer experience challenge.

2 Ensuring the whole organization, not just the few, understands what it means to be design-led.

3 Bringing the right skills in-house.

4 Creativity and bridging the imagination gap.

Connecting the whole organization, not just the few, to the customer experience challenge

There are no longer any organizations we work with in which we find people who don't appreciate that the experiences their customers are having impact the business's bottom line. Yet not every individual has a practical understanding of how their role impacts the customer and many well-intentioned attempts to embed customer experience principles have failed for this reason. It's easy enough to appreciate the role you play if you speak to customers every day. It's easy for those in a marketing role to see the value of a customer-driven proposition and a service that delivers it. It's much harder when you're in a role that's distant from the end customer, when you perceive that you only have 'internal customers'. It's especially hard if your job is explicitly to make or to save as much money as possible for the company. Yet, more of our work is commissioned with the purpose of broadening the extent to which organizations are customer-centred and of taking these perspectives and practical methods to parts of organizations where previously they were seen to have little relevance, for example, in financial management, corporate HR, corporate IT, legal and compliance, procurement or facilities management. Today, we're running projects with such departments and functions to include them in the development of visions for service and in the design of the customer experience. We're also working with functions traditionally distant from end customers to help them interpret the vision and principles in their role. These projects have a dual purpose: to design a better business function, which ultimately improves the experience for customers, and to equip the people who 'are' the service (including the functions invisible to customers) with the understanding and practical approaches needed to play their part.

We're also seeing more mature organizations applying their customer experience design tools and ways of working to the colleague experience and to interdepartmental services and business processes such as procurement, commercial and human resources processes, for example, the recruitment process.

Ensuring the whole organization, not just the few, understands what it means to be design-led

The organizations we work with today are very different from those we worked with when Engine began in 2000 (although ironically some are the same brands, albeit with very different businesses in a very different environment). Back then it was very difficult to get many of those we worked with to appreciate that Design was about more than what something looked like. The need to design websites for the 'World Wide Web' and specifically Steve Jobs and Sir Jonathan Ive changed many businesses' perceptions of the value of Design to business. Yet, Design was still a delivery activity rather than a strategic or organizational one.

The emergence of customer experience as something businesses had to think about meant that the 'experience' became the 'product' and could be considered in the same ways as businesses had previously thought about their products. The customer experience became something that could be designed. This opened the door to the application of tools originally developed for industrial product design and human-computer interface design to the design of services and experiences. The central idea of 'user-centred design' combined with ideas of customer-centred marketing, and design tools combined with marketing ideas (for example, Service Blueprints), to form a new toolkit for customer experience design and a new role for Designers.

Over the last five or six years we realized that designing a new service and experience is relatively easy compared with the challenge of designing a really great one – and more so, making it happen. We also realized that often, by being involved in the design process, the people we were working with changed too. They got excited about being involved and they told us how much more motivated they were by what we were trying to make happen than by any other project they had been asked to contribute to. We began to see the value of the approach and process itself as part of getting new services and experiences out there into the world.

We think we're on to something. Simply put, Design is the considered application of insight and imagination to solving problems and improving the things we do and use. That something works well and looks great is important, but only as a means to an end. The objective of good design is a better way of living. And because this is what it is, design thinking and tools can be used to improve the approaches people take at work as well as the solutions they create. We've seen first-hand how using such tools and working in these ways helps people to think and work differently, not just while they are working with us on projects but in their jobs and with their teams.

The challenge is that this is a very big idea and strays far from many people's experience of Design and of Designers. Promoting this idea more widely in even the more mature organizations will take time. Unfortunately, the Design industry isn't helping to clear up the confusion or make the case for the value of Design beyond its direct role in product development. Many in the Design industry still describe their value solely in terms of the designed 'output', not in the value to the organization of the Design 'process' and tools, nor as a ready-made approach to creative and constructive collaboration across departments and disciplines – a valuable social technology.

Bringing the right skills in-house

As organizations have brought 'Digital' in-house they have – intentionally or not – brought Designers and design thinking in-house too. The ways Designers work and organize their working spaces has started to influence other teams. Many organizations have created Service Design roles in non-digital teams to support proposition and product development. However, these skills are still new and they exist in only a few roles. Design school-trained Designers are being recruited into what could be thought of as non-traditional design roles ('traditional' being, for example, the graphic design or industrial product design department). However, in most cases these Designers have not been recruited into or promoted to senior roles. Many in senior roles still have a limited appreciation of the value of Design and of the Designers they employ. As a result, many of the Designers recruited from an external design agency setting into a corporate one find themselves in an environment that isn't yet able to use their talents fully. Things are changing for the better though, and we're seeing Design teams operate as internal consultancies to many parts of their organization.

Creativity and bridging the imagination gap

This is the hardest challenge of all to crack, even for organizations sailing across the customer-centeredness maturity scale. It's vital to build a robust design process, and the tools described in this book will help immensely. However, there's no getting away from it; challenging and imaginative ideas are needed and these remain hard to summon on demand. More than ideas, organizations often falter because key people struggle to make the leaps of imagination required to appreciate either the problem the organization is facing, or that there might be better ways of serving customers.

In preparation for larger programmes of work with organizations, or at a point when more people need to be involved, we run training workshops in which we train teams in the customer experience design process and the tools we use. As part of this training we often discuss creativity and find ways to make it more accessible to people who don't see themselves as creative. Let's be honest, some people are more creative than others. They just are. But this doesn't mean there aren't things you can do to make original ideas and challenging perspectives more likely, as we explored in Chapter 13, 'Think like a Designer'. Using the tools and asking the questions we've set out in this book are great starting points.

In the true spirit of a self-help manual, the first step is to realize you have a problem, which may mean convincing others in your organization that things need to change for your customers and, by implication, in the way in which you work. We've set out some of the challenges and we've also set out practical responses to these challenges in the form of seven design-led skills. These can be learnt and taught (or bought) and, although we're not suggesting a seven-step process, it's well worth, in the spirit of self-help, tackling them one at a time. And remember, these approaches do make a difference. Go lead.

INDEX